OCEB 2 Certification Guide
Business Process Management - Fundamental Level

Second Edition

T0297778

OCEB 2 Certification Guide
Business Process Management - Fundamental Level

Second Edition

Tim Weilkiens

Christian Weiss

Andrea Grass

Kim Nena Duggen

AMSTERDAM • BOSTON • HEIDELBERG • LONDON
NEW YORK • OXFORD • PARIS • SAN DIEGO
SAN FRANCISCO • SINGAPORE • SYDNEY • TOKYO

Morgan Kaufmann is an imprint of Elsevier

Morgan Kaufmann is an imprint of Elsevier
50 Hampshire Street, 5th Floor, Cambridge, MA 02139, United States

Notices
Knowledge and best practice in this field are constantly changing. As new research and experience broaden
our understanding, changes in research methods, professional practices, or medical treatment may become
necessary.

Practitioners and researchers must always rely on their own experience and knowledge in evaluating and
using any information, methods, compounds, or experiments described herein. In using such information or
methods they should be mindful of their own safety and the safety of others, including parties for whom they
have a professional responsibility.

To the fullest extent of the law, neither the Publisher nor the authors, contributors, or editors, assume any
liability for any injury and/or damage to persons or property as a matter of products liability, negligence or
otherwise, or from any use or operation of any methods, products, instructions, or ideas contained in the
material herein.

Library of Congress Cataloging-in-Publication Data
A catalog record for this book is available from the Library of Congress

British Library Cataloguing-in-Publication Data
A catalogue record for this book is available from the British Library

ISBN: 978-0-12-805352-2

For information on all Morgan Kaufmann publications
visit our website at https://www.elsevier.com/

www.elsevier.com • www.bookaid.org

Working together
to grow libraries in
developing countries

Publisher: Todd Green
Acquisition Editor: Todd Green
Editorial Project Manager: Lindsay Lawrence
Production Project Manager: Priya Kumaraguruparan
Cover Designer: Mark Rogers

Typeset by SPi Global, India

Contents

About the Authors

Tim Weilkiens is member of the board and trainer at oose Innovative Informatik eG. He focuses his work on the modeling of systems, software, and enterprises. He represents oose at OMG and he's the co-developer of the certification program OCEB and OCEB2.
You can contact him at: tim@weilkiens.de

Christian Weiss is managing consultant at Holisticon AG and engages himself as a consultant and coach in business process management, agile project management, and Internet of Things. He particularly focuses on supporting large enterprises in implementing fast, automated business processes, and agile practices.
You can contact him at: cweiss2211@gmail.com

Andrea Grass is a member of oose Innovative Informatik eG. For many years, she has supported enterprises in deploying agile project management. In addition to that, she holds trainings and coachings on business process management and enterprise architectures.
You can contact her at: andrea.grass@gmx.de

Kim Nena Duggen is member of the board and trainer at oose Innovative Informatik eG. Her work focuses on business process management, enterprise architectures, organizational development, and mediation between business and IT.
You can contact her at: kduggen@web.de

Foreword

When our original OCEB BPM certification program was published in 2008, many whom encountered it for the first time—especially business-oriented domain experts—were surprised to see that a technical organization like OMG would support a two-track structure with one side dedicated exclusively to business. Here at OMG, however, we didn't have any trouble with this because we had confidence that the professionals who wrote the original BPMN specification knew the domain well, and had designed this curriculum to fit its needs. Industry response proved them right, of course, and thousands of BPM professionals have taken these exams and become OCEB Certified over the program's lifetime.

But those BPM experts stayed on at OMG to extend BPMN to version 2.0, and that's why we have evolved our program to OCEB 2. We still have business and technical tracks, of course, but the exams now reflect the inclusion in BPMN 2.0 of distributed processes (with collaboration, conversation, and choreography diagrams), project participants represented by Pools, and other changes, as well as industry advances in quality, metrics, and GRC frameworks. Another important addition: At the intermediate level, on both the business and technical sides, you'll encounter decision modeling using OMG's DMN specification—a specification that, although new when these exams were being written, was already noted for its industry impact.

So, as I've already mentioned, we ended up calling the program OCEB—OMG Certified Expert in BPM. But does BPM in this case refer to business process management, or business process modeling? Well, in this case, yes, it does, since the program covers both and, with five examinations and levels has enough space to do the job properly. To see what I'm talking about, take a look at this diagram of the two-track program structure. Most noticeable is the division into business and technical tracks for the upper two levels, but for now we'll focus on the fundamental level at the bottom. It's the subject of this book, of course, but let's consider its importance as a foundation for the upper levels of the program.

You can see the seven major examination topics in the table of contents of this book, or on the OCEB website. They fall into three major categories:

- The business itself
- Business process modeling using BPMN
- Frameworks for process quality, business governance, and metrics

OMG's team of BPM experts included business-oriented topics at this level to ensure that everyone (since this certification is a prerequisite for every other OCEB level) who displays an OCEB certification logo is familiar with the basic concepts of business—goals and objectives, ways and means, and so on—that will be represented in process diagrams and bring in the money to pay everyone's salary. These topics should be familiar to the folks who work on the business side, but will be new to many of the technical people.

Business process modeling using BPMN is well-covered—OMG's team of question-writing experts included many of the principal authors of the BPMN specification itself; senior staff at well-known training companies comprised the rest. Divided into two major topics—BP modeling concepts and BP modeling skills—this part of the certification tests both knowledge of BPMN language elements and, using brief scenarios, familiarity with model-building and model-reading. This level includes only basic parts of BPMN—we've left plenty for the more advanced levels to cover!

The final section, on frameworks for process quality, business governance, and metrics, surveys a range of frameworks that BPM practitioners need to be familiar with. OCEB Certified individuals should be aware of all of these frameworks, since one or another may be helpful, or even necessary in BPM work, depending on one's area of practice. However, this examination does not test the ability to work with any of them—after all, each is (or could be) the subject of its own dedicated certification! At this level, we thought that an awareness of the names, scope, and goals of a wide range of frameworks would provide our certified candidates with the knowledge they need in their practices.

This coverage, and the examination questions themselves, were all written by a team of more than 25 business process management experts and senior trainers listed on the OCEB authors page at http://www.omg.org/oceb/authors.htm. On this page, you'll find the name of Tim Weilkiens, an author of this book. Tim was an active contributor throughout the project, earning the right to display the "OCEB Content Developer" logo on this book. As project leader, I appreciated Tim's timely and high-quality contributions. As a candidate for the OCEB 2 Fundamental certification, you'll appreciate his familiarity with the coverage and material, and ability to collect and digest the many references into a single volume.

As you study your way through this book, and through a course if you've decided to take one, concentrate on developing your BPMN (and BMM!) modeling skills and absorbing the material so you can build your BPM career. Of course you're concerned with "Will this be on the test?," but the question that our team of experts asked before we put anything on the test was "Is this important to the work of a BPM practitioner?," so you can be sure that all of your study will enhance your career as it prepares you for the OCEB Fundamental examination.

Let me personally wish you the best as you prepare to take the OCEB 2 Fundamental examination. I know you'll be proud to display the OCEB 2 Certified logo on your business card and resume, and hope that you'll come back to our program and certify at one or both higher levels in your career track or perhaps even both tracks if your role is BPM Guru.

Jon Siegel, Ph.D.
Vice President, Technology Transfer, and Director Certification OMG,
November 2014

Preface

This book and the certification program, *OMG Certified Expert in Business Process Management 2*, discuss basic knowledge and the concepts of business process management and business process modeling. These are stable and long-term topics. Concrete technologies tend to be instable, and our book contains such a component: the *Business Process Model and Notation*, or BPMN for short.

Five years have passed since the first edition. By then it was already clear that there would be a new version of BPMN. But because changes are always looming on the horizon, this did not prevent OMG from starting the OCEB certification program with the old BPMN in 2010. Nor did it discourage us to write a book on this topic. In 2011, BPMN 2.0 replaced BPMN 1.2.

For almost 2 years, a group of experts has been working on an update of the OCEB certification program, particularly with regard to the update from BPMN1 to BPMN2. Our author, Tim Weilkiens, is a member of this group of experts and contributes to the certification topics and questions. We updated our book in line with the update of the OCEB certification program. It prepares for the initial certification of OCEB2 and imparts basic information on business process management and business process modeling, using BPMN. The book is not only interesting for test preparation, but it also constitutes a compact reference on these topics.

Feedback that we received on the first edition was considered in this second edition. We hope you enjoy reading this book and that it imparts useful information. We look forward to receiving your feedback!

Tim Weilkiens, Christian Weiss, Andrea Grass, Kim Nena Duggen
Hamburg, December 2014

Chapter 1

Getting Started

This is not the end. It is not even the beginning of the end.
But it is, perhaps, the end of the beginning.

Winston Churchill

1.1 SENSE AND NONSENSE OF CERTIFICATIONS

As you are holding this book in your hands, you presumably think that certifications make sense. At least in the certification of *OMG Certified Expert in Business Process Management 2* (OCEB2) of *Object Management Group* (OMG). The subject of certification is discussed rather controversially and emotionally. The goal of this section is to take an objective look at the pros and cons of certifications. The subsequent sections are then dedicated to the OCEB2 certification and its contents.

Types of Tests

The arguments in favor and against certifications are representative for certificates with automated tests without any initial requirements. Certificates that not only examine knowledge, but also test skills, for instance, in the course of an oral examination, or by demanding initial requirements, like proof of practical experience, may have different arguments.

Measuring Knowledge

These certificates basically involve a measurable proof of knowledge. Let's assume you want to hire consultants in the area of business process management (BPM). How do you determine beforehand which BPM knowledge the people have? Associate degrees prove holistic skills rather than topic-specific knowledge, such as BPM. An OCEB2 certificate is a tiny little piece of the answer to this question. Of course, you must not consider the certificate separately, and even less does it replace a one-to-one interview.

OCEB 2 Certification Guide. http://dx.doi.org/10.1016/B978-0-12-805352-2.00001-7

Forgetting Knowledge

Knowledge is subject to half-life. You forget things that you don't use regularly. For this reason, there are certificates that have an expiration date. After this expiration date, you must repeat the examination and pay for it to renew the certificate. This is very profitable for those issuing the certificates, and everyone may have their own opinion to what extent these repeated examinations make sense, for instance, for pilot licenses, or whether the date of the first examination, and some knowledge on the projects implemented are sufficient to get a good idea of how up-to-date the knowledge actually is. The OCEB2 certificates are valid for 5 years. This expiration is printed on your certificate.

Knowledge versus Skills

In real life, certificates are frequently misinterpreted and occasionally misused. Someone who doesn't know anything about the content or implementation of a certificate may easily be misled by alleged knowledge, skills, and experience, which most certificates don't prove at all. For example, an analyst requires the ability to abstract, have analytic power, excellent communication skills, and other soft skills. These skills are not covered by the OCEB2 certificates, and they could not be checked by any other multiple-choice test. This way, skills can only be verified to a limited extent or not at all. A certificate like OCEB2 is only a measure of knowledge—no more, no less.

Demand

It can be clearly perceived that the demand for certificates has increased in recent years. Certificates exist because there's a requirement for them. They don't grow on trees. One of the requirements has been shown previously: The requirement to make knowledge measurable. But there are further interests and the associated stakeholders.

Increasing the Value

The person certified possibly doesn't want to be measured at all. Maybe he wants to use the certificate to increase his value in order to increase his prospects for a good job or a profitable assignment. Or he perceives the certificate as a privilege. Email signatures frequently provide a proud list of all certificates achieved.

Supervisors

Supervisors are also stakeholders in the certification business. Maybe they want to use the certifications to upgrade their teams to the outside to be more successful in customer acquisition. As trainers for various certifications, we often witness that supervisors want to use certifications to test their employees, or make target agreements that are relevant for their salary. When the participants introduce themselves during our preparatory course they often say: "My boss wants me to do this." Sometimes, there are also managers who don't pay their employees' certification because they dread fluctuation or higher salary demands due to the gain in status of the employee.

Commerce

The list of stakeholders wouldn't be complete without the certification organization itself. For OCEB2, these include OMG and *UML Technology Institute* (UTI) that developed the certification program and assume responsibility for it. There is no financial interest here. The revenues are to cover the costs for developing the certificate. However, OMG provides certificates to enable its members to earn money, for instance, with preparatory courses and consulting services in the topic area of the respective certificate. Persons running test centers also earn money. All examinations of OMG, and thus OCEB2, are done in *Pearson VUE* test centers.

A certificate is only one tiny little option of many others to assess a person. Depending on the context, it can be an important or unimportant little piece or simply the final touch to round off a person's image.

1.2 **THE OCEB2 CERTIFICATION PROGRAM**

The certification program, OCEB2, offers five certificates that prove expertise in the BPM area. It is the third certification program of OMG after the OCUP[1] and OCRES[2] certification programs. The standardization consortium is primarily associated with UML,[3] MDA,[4] and CORBA.[5] That's where you can find the roots of OMG. In the meantime, however, a considerable tree of standards has grown out of other areas. Besides systems

---

[1] OMG Certified UML Professional.

[2] OMG Certified Real-time and Embedded Specialist.

[3] Unified Modeling Language.

[4] Model Driven Architecture.

[5] Common Object Request Broker Architecture.

engineering with OMG SysML,[6] the consortium has also discovered the discipline of business process management. OMG is responsible for many significant standards from this area, including *Business Process Model and Notation* (BPMN), *Business Process Maturity Model* (BPMM), and *Business Motivation Model* (BMM).

Goal

These and other BPM standards provide support to discover, incorporate, optimize, and implement business processes. The goal of OCEB2 is to provide a measure for this knowledge [18].

Developers

The certification program has been developed by a team of international experts. These include, for example, the OMG's project leader, Jon Siegel, Stephen White[7] from IBM, as well as several employees from oose. You can find a full list of participants on OCEB2's official website: http://www.omg.org/oceb-2 [19].

Contents

OCEB2 not only addresses standards of OMG, but also asks questions on general knowledge of project and business process management, business administration, and basic rules, or quality frameworks like Six Sigma.

Accordingly, the reference list not only comprises OMG specifications, but also various articles and books. The list is rather comprehensive because, so far, no individual book has been published that covers such a wide range of topics in the area of business processes. But don't worry: Only individual sections from the many books are referenced and not all hundreds of pages. Moreover, you are holding this preparatory book in your hands that fully covers the topics relevant for *OCEB2 Fundamental*. You only require the official references if you want to read the original or require additional information.

Certificates

There are five OCEB2 certificates in total (Table 1.1). The *Fundamental* level covers basic knowledge. This forms the basis from where OCEB2 branches to a technical and a business area. The technical certificates are intended for IT employees who implement business processes in systems, that is, architects, designers, and developers. Topics include, for example,

---

[6]OMG Systems Modeling Language.

[7]Stephen White is considered as one of the fathers of BPMN.

Table 1.1 OCEB2 Certification Program		
OCEB Profile		
Name	OMG Certified Expert in Business Process Management 2	
Target group	Business analysts and architects, software designers and developers	
Levels	*Business Advanced*	*Technical Advanced*
	Business Intermediate	*Technical Intermediate*
	Fundamental	
Prerequisites	None	
Test environment	Pearson VUE test center	
	Multiple choice	
	Language: English	
Validity	Expires after 5 years	
	Identical on an international scale	

detailed modeling aspects, information security, and architectures such as *Service Oriented Architecture* (SOA). The business certificates address analysts, architects, and also employees of specialist departments. Topics comprise, for example, *change management*, process improvement, or the management of business processes.

The following sections briefly present the individual levels. As of Chapter 2, we only deal with the topics of the Fundamental level.

1.2.1 **OCEB2 Fundamental**

The lowest level of the certification program bridges the gap between the IT department and the analyst teams, or specialist departments. It creates a uniform understanding for terms, concepts, methods, and modeling of business processes. The following topic areas are covered. The percentages each indicate the weighting in the certification process.

Topics
- Business goals, objectives (8%)
- Business process concepts and fundamentals (11%)
- Business process management concepts and fundamentals (10%)
- Business motivation modeling (16%)
- Business process modeling concepts (24%)

- Business process modeling skills (16%)
- Process quality, governance, and metrics frameworks (15%)

Business Goals

The *business goals* topic area entails concepts of business administration, marketing, and project management. Anyone who works in the business process environment should have basic knowledge of organizational forms of enterprises, market environment analyses, marketing, financial key figures, and business analysis methods.

Business Processes

Independent of the standard BPMN, the two topic areas, *concepts and fundamentals of business processes* and *concepts and fundamentals of business process management*, require basic knowledge of business processes. Not only the What, but also the How is important, for example, how to discover business processes or present business process hierarchies, and how to handle the various degrees of abstraction in the description. By aligning the business processes with the business goals, a link is established between the first and the third topic areas.

BPM

The *business process management concepts and fundamentals* topic area deals with the handling of business processes in enterprises, the impacts of process-focused structures, and the various approaches of business process management such as *Business Process Reengineering* (BPR) or *Total Quality Management* (TQM). Another topic is again an OMG standard: *Business Process Maturity Model* (BPMM). This is a maturity model for business processes similar to *Capability Maturity Model Integration* (CMMI) for software and system development.

BMM

The *business motivation modeling* topic area addresses another OMG specifications. The *Business Motivation Model* (BMM) is a standard to describe business plans. It defines the basic artifacts, their characteristics, and their interrelationship. This includes vision, mission, strategy, business rules, objectives, influencers, and appraisals.

BPMN

With a total of 40%, the *business process modeling concepts and skills* topic assumes the largest part of the *OCEB2-Fundamental* certification. The OMG standard, BPMN, predominates here. BPMN fundamentals and the diagram elements of the process diagram are required here. You not only need to know what a specific element represents, but also must be able to interpret a BPMN diagram. You must be able to answer contextual questions on a process diagram with real subject-matter knowledge.

Frameworks
The last topic area of the OCEB2 Fundamental certification deals with *process quality*, *governance*, and *metrics frameworks*.

1.2.2 **OCEB2 Business Intermediate**

This branch addresses the business world of business processes with digressions to the technical implementation of business processes.

The *Business Intermediate* level comprises six topic areas:

Topics
- Intermediate business motivational modeling (10%)
- Business process modeling with BPMN (35%)
- Decision management and modeling with DMN (10%)
- Business rules approach and shared business-wide vocabulary (10%)
- Business process management knowledge and skills (20%)
- Process quality and governance frameworks (15%)

1.2.3 **OCEB Business Advanced**

The business advanced and the two technical exams were not updated from OCEB to OCEB2 when this book was written.

The *Business Advanced* level also comprises six topic areas:

Topics
- Advanced business process modeling with BPMN (15%)
- Aligning BPM with enterprise goals and resources (11%)
- Management of BPM programs (27%)
- Advanced *change management* (11%)
- *Compliance* and *assurance* (22%)
- Advanced topics in process improvement (14%)

1.2.4 **OCEB Technical Intermediate**

This branch addresses the technical world of business processes, for instance, application architectures such as SOA or workflow management systems. Here you can also find topics of the business branch, whereas the focus is on the technology now. OCEB2 thus bridges these two worlds by certifying a common understanding of the terminology used.

The *Technical Intermediate* level comprises seven topic areas:

Topics
- Business process management awareness (10%)
- Business process modeling with BPMN (31%)
- Workflow pattern (7%)
- Business rules (16%)
- Architecture topics (13%)
- IT infrastructure and business process (13%)
- Monitoring and managing processes (10%)

1.2.5 **OCEB Technical Advanced**

The *Technical Advanced* level also covers seven topic areas:

Topics
- Business process management awareness (13%)
- Advanced business process modeling with BPMN (25%)
- Business rules (8%)
- Understanding metamodeling concepts (9%)
- Enterprise architecture (23%)
- Implementation and integration (9%)
- Vendor selection and marketplace topics (13%)

1.3 **OBJECT MANAGEMENT GROUP**

This section briefly introduces you to the organization that stands behind the OCEB2 certification program.

OMG is an international standardization organization. Since 1989, it has developed and managed standards in various disciplines and domains such as software development, systems engineering, GPM, financials, authorities, healthcare, robotics, and many more. The best-known standards include are CORBA,[8] UML, OMG SysML, and BPMN.

Members
Any organization can join OMG and actively participate in the standardization process. Almost all large enterprises of the IT industry and many small companies as well as universities are represented in OMG.

Meetings
Each year, OMG organizes conferences and *technical meetings*, where the various task teams come together to discuss and adopt standards.

---

[8]Common Object Request Broker Architecture.

Certifications

With the implementation of UML 2.0 in 2003, OMG for the first time developed a certification program called OCUP to provide a scale for the knowledge about one of its standards. This was followed by OCRES in 2006 for standards and general knowledge in the area of embedded systems. OCEB was developed and published as the third certification program in 2008. Additionally, OCSMP has been available for systems modeling since 2010.

1.4 **CERTIFICATION PROCESS**

Figure 1.1 depicts the certification process in a comprehensive form.

Coverage Map

The first step on the path to certification is the contextual preparation. The topics covered by the certification are specified by OMG in the *coverage map* (Section A.1). The spectrum of topics is very diversified. Accordingly, the list of books, articles, and specifications, which are part of the official reference list of *OCEB2 Fundamental*, is very long. It takes a lot of effort to read and understand all of these references. And it also involves some rather significant costs, which will make the bookseller of your choice very happy. We've prepared these topics in a compressed form and have written this book on the basic knowledge for business process management.

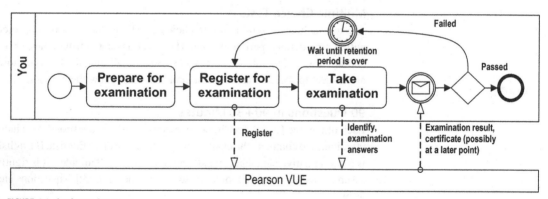

■ **FIGURE 1.1** Certification Process

Experience

Furthermore, we, as the authors of this book, have extensive experience with the OCEB2 certification. oose employees even participated in the development of the tests. They concerned themselves with the topic coverage and are authors of numerous original questions. Oose was the first enterprise in

Germany to offer preparatory courses. This way, we were able to get profound insight in the experiences of our participants.

We compiled this information in this book. Note, however, that although we know the concrete questions, we won't pass them on because then the test and the certificate would become worthless. In addition, this is illegal. It is therefore not sufficient to just read this book or learn everything by heart—this book is supposed to be a guide to understand the BPM basic knowledge.

Registration

Taking the examination is the easiest step on the road to the OCEB2 certification. Go to the website of OMG certification at Pearson VUE, http://www.pearsonvue.com/omg, search for a test center nearby, and register for an exam. Specific professional prerequisites, such as a university degree, are not necessary. The examination fee amounts to ~$200.

Exam

You must take a computer-based exam to obtain OCEB2 certificates. Participants must report to the test center, have a picture taken, and identify themselves before the test begins. Formally, two IDs (e.g., an ID card and driver's license) are required. One of these IDs must have a photograph. At the test center, the participants are briefly instructed on how to use the test software. Then the test starts, and the countdown begins.

Multiple-Choice Tests

The test includes several multiple-choice questions that must be answered within a predefined period of time. The questions come from a large pool and are always recombined so that the tests are all unique. The questions are subject to secrecy, and the test center doesn't know them either.

90 Questions in 90+30 Minutes

Each of the five OCEB2 certification exams entails 90 questions. You have 90 minutes to complete the exam. The questions are all in English. If English is not your native language, you are granted another 30 minutes. It is rightly assumed that you require more time to understand the English questions and answers.

Each question is provided on a separate screen, and you can scroll back and forth between the questions. It is useful to answer the questions in the given sequence, but you can also skip questions and answer them later on. You have the option to set a little flag for each question. You can then do an overview to see which questions still need to be answered, and for which questions you've set a flag.

Test Questions

At the end of the respective chapters of this book, you can find a set of test questions that are similar to the original questions of the certification. These enable you to get a feel for the type of questions, and you can check your current state of knowledge.

Surveillance

The test room is under video surveillance or monitored directly by test center staff. It is not permitted to take along any aids, even paper or pens are not allowed. The test center provides memo means, which must be returned after completion. If participants break these rules, they automatically fail. The persons running the test center are also subject to strict requirements and controls.

Certificate

You pass the *Fundamental* exam if you've answered at least 62 out of 90 questions correctly (~69%). Other values apply for the subsequent OCEB2 certificates. The result is available immediately, and—if you passed—you receive a preliminary certificate to take along with you. The official document—in color for the picture frame behind your desk—is delivered by mail later on.

Fail and Repeat: Retention Period

If you've failed a test, you must wait at least 30 days to repeat the exam. A maximum of three attempts is permitted within 12 months.

The five certification levels are based on one another, that is, you only obtain a higher certificate if you've successfully passed the previous one. So it is not possible to only pass the *OCEB Business Advanced* test to receive the certificate.

Knowledge Transfer

Also plan to transfer your acquired knowledge into practice. In the short term, your only goal is to pass the exam, but surely you also have medium-term goals with regard to contents. You invest a lot of energy to build up this knowledge. Utilize this basis to improve yourself in practice. The best way to preserve theoretical knowledge is to use it in practice.

1.4.1 **Case Study**

In this book, we often refer to the case study of the company, *SpeedyCar*, to explain the topics with a practical orientation. To understand the context, the following briefly introduces this example.

The car rental company, *SpeedyCar*,[9] has set the goal to minimize employment of staff with innovative IT systems and thus, be able to offer unbeatable prices in the market. Of course, the service must not fall by the wayside. Quite the contrary: The service is supposed to be considerably better and more apparent to customers, compared to competitors. One specific feature of SpeedyCar is that only registered customers can utilize the services. In return, they receive particularly favorable prices toward conventional car rental companies.

SpeedyCar commissions oose[10] to perform an actual and target analysis of the business and the processes. The results form the basis for the future strategic orientation of the company.

The actual and target analysis is not discussed continuously in this book, but we will focus on the contents of the *OCEB2 Fundamental* certification and show sections that depict the current topic.

1.4.2 **Thank You!**

Thank You, OMG!

The constructive arguments within OMG during the development of the certification program with experts from around the world have ensured a lot of "aha" experiences. Our special thanks go to Jon Siegel, who runs the OCEB2 certification program and wrote the Preface to this book.

Thank You, oose!

The environment and the freedom that oose gives us are very important for our further professional and personal development. Many thanks go to our coworkers. Some figures of this book are by courtesy of oose.

Thank You, Publisher!

Great praise and big thank you is due to the publisher, dpunkt.verlag and particularly to Christa Preisendanz!

---

[9]*SpeedyCar* is a purely fictional company.

[10]oose is not fictional. You can find it at http://www.oose.de.

Thank You, Reviewer!

A book can never achieve good quality without a qualified review. A view from the outside is essential. In this context, we'd like to thank our coworkers and Ms. Bühlmann from Switzerland for her suggestions.

ADDITIONAL REFERENCES

[1] OMG: http://www.omg.org—main page of OMG, http://www.omg.org/oceb-2/—official OCEB2 pages of OMG.

[2] E-mail contact to the authors: cweiss2211@gmail.com, tim@larus.de, andrea.grass@gmx.de, kduggen@web.de.

[3] Consulting and seminars on BPM: http://www.oose.de.

Chapter 2

Basic Principles of Business Management

Manager: The man who knows exactly what he cannot do, and finds the right persons to do it for him.

Philip Rosenthal

OCEB2 REFERENCE

Steven Stralser, MBA in a Day [35]; Tim Gorman, The Complete Idiot's Guide to MBA Basics [17].

The term *business* is already included in the name of the OCEB2 certification. And as the structure of the certification program already suggests, it is particularly important to the persons behind this idea to establish a common language between experts and IT employees. This is reason enough to deal with the basics of business management and get acquainted with some basic terminology and concepts of this economic science—at least from the business process perspective.[1]

2.1 BUSINESS FUNCTIONS, MARKETS, AND STRATEGIES

Developing strategies in line with market requirements is not as easy as it seems. This entails some strategic deliberations and careful investigations of the market environment, as well as a straightforward consideration of your own strengths and weaknesses.

---

[1]At this point, we would like to apologize to all business economists: We are well aware that the concepts presented here are not remotely sufficient for discussions among laymen—but it's a first step.

OCEB 2 Certification Guide. http://dx.doi.org/10.1016/B978-0-12-805352-2.00002-9

2.1.1 **Typical Business Functions**

Usually, an enterprise has a lot to do to accomplish its purpose. If you very roughly group these tasks, you obtain *business functions* that are very similar in most enterprises (Figure 2.1).

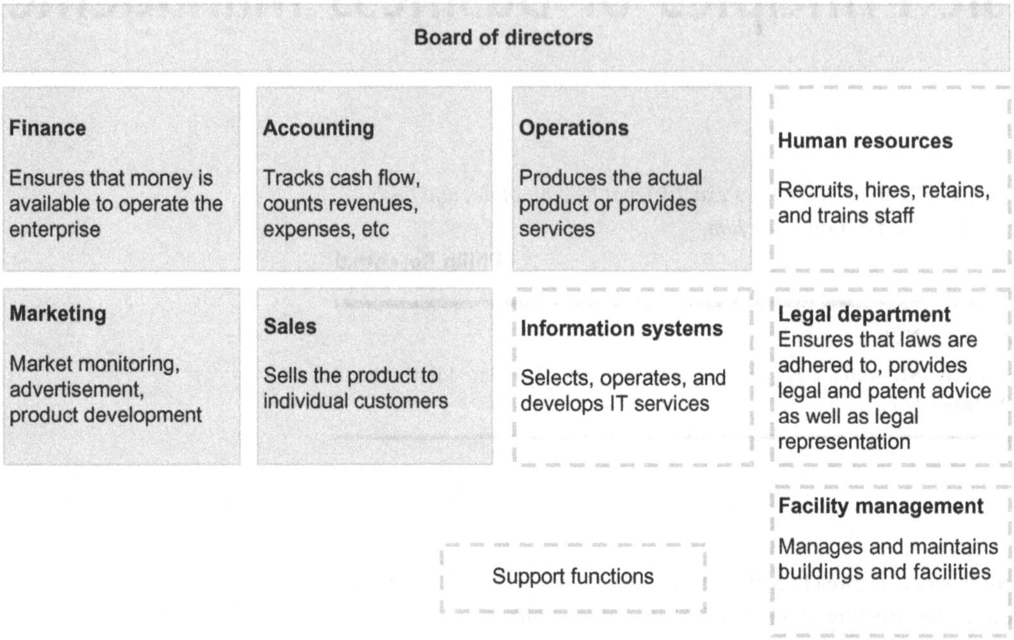

Board of directors			
Finance Ensures that money is available to operate the enterprise	**Accounting** Tracks cash flow, counts revenues, expenses, etc	**Operations** Produces the actual product or provides services	**Human resources** Recruits, hires, retains, and trains staff
Marketing Market monitoring, advertisement, product development	**Sales** Sells the product to individual customers	**Information systems** Selects, operates, and develops IT services	**Legal department** Ensures that laws are adhered to, provides legal and patent advice as well as legal representation
		Support functions	**Facility management** Manages and maintains buildings and facilities

■ **FIGURE 2.1** Typical Business Functions

Business Function versus Department

Even if you have this impression: Business functions are not departments because a *department* can execute multiple functions. In enterprises with traditional organization, however, it is often common practice to establish a department for more or less one particular function. Therefore, department and function are often used synonymously. In modern and rather process-oriented enterprises, however, a function is frequently mapped onto multiple organization units.

Core and Support Functions

Depending on whether a business function directly serves the object of the enterprise or not, you can distinguish *core functions* or *support functions*.

Reflect on the typical enterprise functions of Figure 2.1 for a while and particularly memorize the terms of the functions and the tasks associated with them.

Human Resources

Special attention should be paid to *human resources*. Apart from the vision of a fully electronic enterprise where only robots work,[2] the employees (and who should know that better than you, dear reader) are the ones that enable an enterprise in the first place to implement its strategies. Nevertheless, human resources are usually considered as a support function.

2.1.2 **Managers and Their Competencies**

What does a manager actually do all day long? Of course, OCEB2s cannot answer this question in your context, but they know some basic terms for this.

DEFINITION

The term *management* is kind of old (Latin *mansionem agere* = the house order) and describes the process of letting things happen by others.

An alternative common definition is: *"Management is what managers do."*

Manager Delegate

So it's not important what is actually organized. The main thing is that others do it.

DEFINITION

As a result, a *manager* is a person who organizes, plans, supports, defines, and assesses the work of others.

If you now look at a whole enterprise, another term is often used in literature:

DEFINITION

Business administration is understood as controlling and organizing business activities.

Seven Manager Competencies

A manager requires certain key competencies to let wondrous things happen by others. To be more precise, a manager requires seven competencies:

- *Goal setting*
- *Planning*

---

[2]Except for the owner, of course.

- *Decision-making*
- *Delegation*
- *Support*
- *Communication*
- *Controlling*

2.1.3 **Business Strategies**

Surely, you've played chess before. The goal is kind of clear: win. But what's the best strategy? As you know, there are countless possibilities. Once you've decided on a strategy, you move your chessmen in compliance with this strategy. You do so until you're convinced that another strategy would be more clever.

The Strategy is the Means to an End

This similarly applies to the business strategy. It is always a means to the business end and must match the enterprise's mission (Chapter 5 distinguishes the terms, vision, mission, goal, strategy, and tactic in more detail).

The business strategy, as long as it is valid, defines the direction into which an organization develops. It thus provides a framework for decisions, similar to guardrails on the highway that ensure that all cars are driving in the same direction, at least between two exits.

To yield an advantage within the changing market environment, it is occasionally necessary to change the strategy in order to newly configure the organization's resources.

As soon as the enterprise's strategy has been defined, you can derive various factors (e.g., personnel and marketing strategy, goals). The enterprise's personnel require goals so that they can align their actions and consider them in the overall context (business strategy). Actively defined goals motivate the people, and the consolidation of contradictory goals across various departments to create similarities.

2.1.4 **Strategy Development**

If a chess player wants to decide on a strategy, he surely doesn't do so without due consideration. Instead, he will gather some information, particularly about his opponent. Presumably, he'll take a look at the games of chess he already played to determine a pattern and detect strengths and weaknesses.

Business Strategy Steps

That's what an enterprise basically does to determine its business strategy:

- First, it analyzes the market environment. (Which forces affect the market? Which factors influence the strategy selection?)
- Then, it divides the market into segments theoretically. (Which buyer groups exist? Where are any market niches?)
- Then, the enterprise analyzes its strengths and weaknesses, if required, for each market segment separately.
- This forms the basis for *setting objectives* and planning the measures to be taken.

Signs like failures, times absent, and fluctuation or large amounts of over-time indicate that the enterprise's personnel management must be adapted. In the best case, this is done based on the strategy. After the strategy has been developed, you can and should plan the personnel deployment by analyzing various aspects:

- Strategic vision of the enterprise.
- Short-term and long-term goals.
- Changes in the market that impact the enterprise.
- Requirements with regard to personnel based on the strategic vision.
- Possible opposition in the organization.

Beyond personnel management, it makes sense to break down the enterprise strategy into goals. These goals (or targeted conditions) should reflect the enterprise strategy and support orientation and optimization when assigned to individual business processes.

After the internal view, the following discusses the market analysis, that is, if you continue reading you get to know some customary techniques to implement these steps.

2.1.5 **Porters Five Forces**

Michael E. Porter is one of the leading economists in the area of strategic management and, for many years, he has occupied himself with how enterprises can gain a competitive edge. He developed the *Porter's Five Forces* framework that supports an enterprise in selecting a suitable strategy to gain a competitive edge.

Market Structure

The idea is simple: The enterprise's success significantly depends on the competitive strategy which is mainly determined by the structure of the market in which the enterprise is active. The market structure of an industry can be attractive or not. But which forces impact this industry structure and thus the attractiveness of a market? (Figure 2.2).

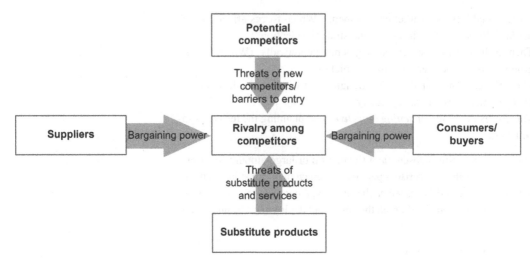

■ **FIGURE 2.2** Porter's Five Forces

Porter's Five Forces

The following five forces exist:

- *Rivalry among competitors*,
- If an enterprise is already in the market: *threats of new competitors*, or if the enterprise wants to enter a new market: *barriers to entry*,
- *Bargaining power of consumers/buyers*,
- *Threats of substitute products or services*, and
- *Bargaining power of suppliers*.

It is obvious that enterprises should attempt to be active in an industry whose market structure is exposed to as few threats from these forces as possible.

2.1.6 **STEP Analysis**

STEP = PEST

Another option to analyze and assess the attractiveness of a market is to use the STEP analysis (Figure 2.3). The acronym consists of the initial letters of the market environment factors to be considered (this technique is also referred to as PEST analysis[3]).

---

[3]Different sorting of the terms.

Sociological/demographic factors	Technological factors
■ Values ■ Lifestyle ■ Demographic influencers ■ Income distribution ■ Education ■ Population growth ■ Safety	■ Research and development ■ New products and processes ■ Product lifecycles ■ Public research expenditure
Economic factors	Political factors
■ Economic growth ■ Inflation ■ Interest rates ■ Exchange rates ■ Taxation ■ Unemployment ■ Business cycles ■ Availability of resources	■ Competition with authorities ■ Legislation ■ Political stability ■ Governance principles ■ Trade barriers ■ Safety directives ■ Subsidies

■ **FIGURE 2.3** STEP Analysis

Ready-Made System

This ready-made system simply provides references for considering the opportunities and threats of a market. For example, an enterprise can consider which threats it is exposed to with regard to the trend of interest rates. Likewise, there can be opportunities, for instance, if the enterprise can manufacture products that are subsidized.

2.1.7 **Market Segmentation**

Isemarkt in Hamburg

Have you ever been to the Isemarkt in the German Hanseatic City of Hamburg? This is a rather big weekly market that spreads almost half a mile below the city's metro rails. Various market segments, such as jewelry stands, vegetable stands, and so on, exist there. The attractiveness of the market doesn't necessarily depend on the whole market, but on the competitive situation in the respective segment.[4]

---

[4]Personally, we usually use the "lunch" segment.

This does not only apply to weekly markets. For this reason, a complete market for products and services is usually subdivided into small, manageable segments. The heterogeneous total quantity of market participants is divided into homogeneous target groups which market policy efforts should focus on (Figure 2.4).

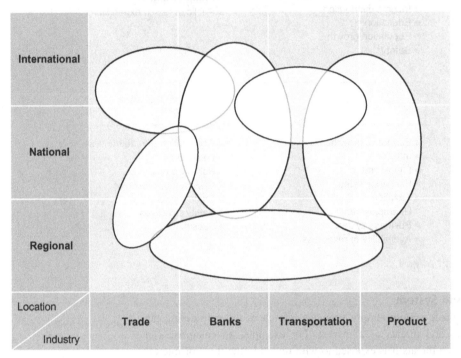

■ **FIGURE 2.4** Market Segmentation

Division Strategies for Market Segments

There are various division strategies for the segmentation of a market:

- One-dimensional segmentation, for instance, by income classes,
- Multidimensional segmentation, for instance, by countries and income classes, and
- Complete segmentation where each customer is handled individually.

Market Niches

Because not every segment entails the same profitability, market niches can arise. They provide an opportunity to gain the leadership in the market segment.

2.1.8 **SWOT Analysis**

The previously described techniques (Porter's Five Forces, STEP analysis, and market segmentation) help to analyze the market environment externally, that is, the environment outside an enterprise. It makes you realize which *opportunities* and *threats* exist with regard to a market or market segment.

Derive Strengths and Weaknesses

But not only is the market environment of an enterprise of interest, but also the enterprise itself. It has specific characteristics (for instance, quality of products compared to competitors, qualification of employees, level of awareness) with which it acts within the market. Within the scope of an internal analysis, these characteristics can be used to derive *strengths* and *weaknesses* of the enterprise, with regard to a market or market segment.

The collected results of the external and internal analysis can be initially presented as an overview using a SWOT matrix (Figure 2.5).

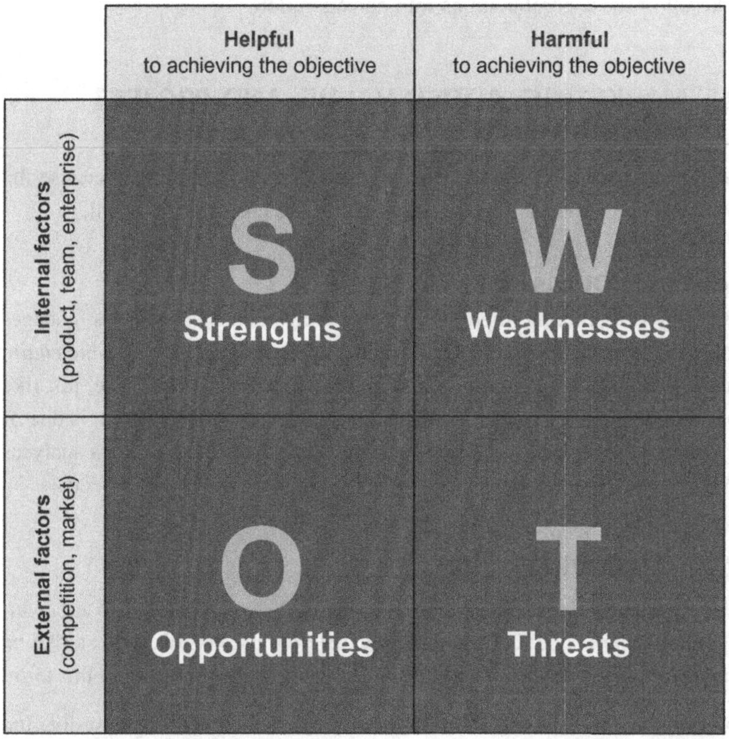

	Helpful to achieving the objective	**Harmful** to achieving the objective
Internal factors (product, team, enterprise)	**S** **Strengths**	**W** **Weaknesses**
External factors (competition, market)	**O** **Opportunities**	**T** **Threats**

■ **FIGURE 2.5** SWOT Matrix

This summarizing comparison often helps you to think about how you can leverage strengths and decrease weaknesses in order to pursue opportunities in a targeted manner and avert threats.

Four Combinations

When you compare the results of the internal analysis with the result of the external analysis, you obtain four combinations that form a holistic business strategy:

- Strengths + opportunities: Pursue new opportunities that blend well with the strengths of the enterprise.
- Strengths + threats: Leverage strengths to avert threats.
- Weaknesses + opportunities: Decrease weaknesses to leverage new opportunities.
- Weaknesses + threats: Develop defense strategies so that weaknesses don't result in threats.

Because each enterprise has both strengths and weaknesses, and each market environment involves both opportunities and threats, you should always take all of these combinations into consideration.

2.2 MARKETING, ADDED VALUE, AND PROJECT MANAGEMENT

Marketing is of high significance in virtually every enterprise because the products and services must be delivered to the customer, after all.

Marketing Designs the Value Chain

But why is marketing important for an expert in business process management? One of the most important business process types is the *value chain*. It's one of marketing's tasks to design the value chain. Therefore, just like basic knowledge of project management, understanding this term is one of the basic competencies of a BPM expert, because business process analyses and business process optimizations are typically handled in projects.

2.2.1 Marketing

The term *marketing* is not as clear as it seems. A good business process management expert should therefore know different uses of this term so that he can distinguish them in heated discussions and ask how others use this term.

A common, rather business-related definition is that marketing describes the orientation of an enterprise in the market:

DEFINITION

Marketing is the market-oriented realization of enterprise goals and the alignment of the entire enterprise in the market.

The subsequent advanced, and rather economical, definition understands marketing as a global event and therefore focuses not only on the individual enterprise, but also the interactions in the markets:

DEFINITION

Marketing is a process in the economic and social structure which individuals and groups use to meet their requirements and requests by generating, offering, and exchanging products and other things of value.

Forms of Marketing

However you interpret marketing, you can run "marketing" either reactively or proactively. Consequently, you can distinguish two different forms of marketing (Figure 2.6).

■ **FIGURE 2.6** Forms of Marketing

Reactive and Proactive

An enterprise uses reactive marketing if it (only) reacts to what others do and imitates them. Proactive marketing, by contrast, is a philosophy which ensures that resources are deployed in such a way that the requests, requirements, and needs of customers take center stage in the enterprise's activity.

2.2.2 **Process Elements of Marketing**

If you understand marketing as a business process (Chapter 3), this inevitably raises the question of which elements or activities this process generally involves.

Marketing ≠ Brochures and Trade Fairs

Marketing is by no means limited to designing brochures and attending trade fairs. This understanding involves a very manifold and continuous process that ultimately touches most enterprise areas (Figure 2.7).

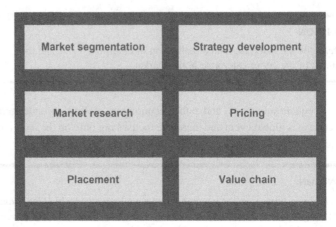

■ **FIGURE 2.7** Overview of Process Elements of Marketing

2.2.3 **Value Chain**

One term that often comes up in the context of marketing and business processes is *value chain*. Michael E. Porter—whom you already know from Figure 2.2—wrote the following on this topic [28]:

DEFINITION

Every enterprise is a collection of activities that are performed to design, produce, market, deliver, and support its product. All these activities can be represented in a *value chain*.

Figure 2.8 shows a typical value chain.

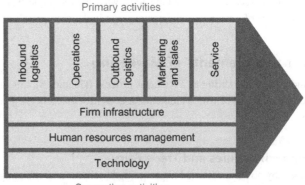

■ **FIGURE 2.8** Typical Value Chain

Primary and Supporting Processes

Most notations of value chains typically use arrows to distinguish between *core processes* (also primary processes or activities) and *supporting processes*. Let's take a closer look at the eight individual elements of the value chain (*inbound* and *outbound logistics*, and so on). They are indeed typical, even if you don't find the processes mentioned there in exactly this form in every enterprise, or if they have other names.

2.2.4 **Projects**

Many plans in the environment of business process management are handled as projects. It is therefore expected from a BPM expert that he (or she) knows what a project actually is.

What a Project is

Perhaps, you are currently in a project or know from other sources that a project:

- is an undertaking with limited timeframes and budget to deliver several clearly defined results and
- is basically characterized by the uniqueness of conditions in their entirety.

Great! Then we don't have to write this down now. By the time you encounter certification questions on this topic, you will remember: Projects are limited and unique.

2.2.5 **Project Management**

Well, we've already discussed what management is (remember: Letting things happen by others or "*what managers do*"). Applied to a project, this means:

DEFINITION

Project management is the application of knowledge, skills, tools, and techniques on a set of activities to meet a specified objective [35].

At first, this sounds trivial. In reality, of course, this process involves a good deal of different tasks, which can be grouped as shown in Figure 2.9.

In this presentation, project management already starts with the *initiation* of the project. The project itself does not start until the project charter has been signed. This is followed by *planning*, *executing*, and *controlling* the project.

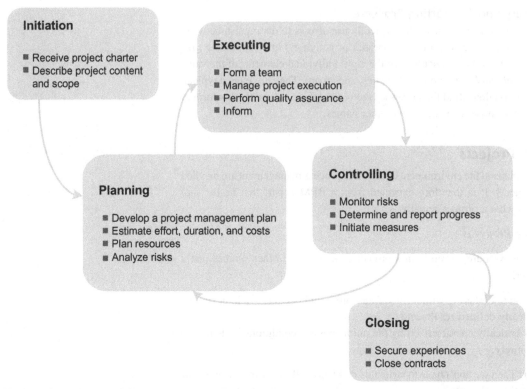

Initiation

- Receive project charter
- Describe project content and scope

Executing

- Form a team
- Manage project execution
- Perform quality assurance
- Inform

Planning

- Develop a project management plan
- Estimate effort, duration, and costs
- Plan resources
- Analyze risks

Controlling

- Monitor risks
- Determine and report progress
- Initiate measures

Closing

- Secure experiences
- Close contracts

■ **FIGURE 2.9** Project Management Tasks

Usually, changes arise from controlling so that the cycle starts all over again. The final step of the project is referred to as *closing*.

2.3 **EFFORTS AND KEY FIGURES**

The basic knowledge of business management naturally also includes efforts and key figures.

2.3.1 **Cost Types**

Fixed, Variable, and Overhead Costs
In the most general sense, you must be able to distinguish at least fixed, variable, and overhead costs.

DEFINITION

Fixed costs are costs that are constant within a specific period of time and are independent of the production volume or quantity of sales.

Do you have a car? Excellent[5] Then, car taxes and insurance are the essential fixed costs. They incur independently of the mileage, even if you leave your (licensed) car in garage.

DEFINITION

Variable costs are costs that vary if the production volume or quantity of sales changes.

In our car example, these are primarily operating costs, mainly for gas. The more miles you drive, the higher the variable costs are.

DEFINITION

Overhead costs are costs that can be allocated only indirectly to a cost unit (product, service).

If you had an entire car pool to rent instead of a single car, then costs for personnel or garages or, electricity and water cannot be allocated to a car according to the cost-by-cause principle, but must be distributed to all vehicles.[6]

2.3.2 **Financial Key Figures**

Besides the general distinction of cost types, there are numerous financial key figures out of which only a few are significant within the scope of the OCEB2 certification.

Working Capital

But how does an enterprise actually know whether it is able to meet its obligations? In principle, it's very simple: It measures the (more or less) available capital.

---

[5]If not, you can surely use your imagination.

[6]You experience this every year when your landlord sends the bill for utility costs, in which the overhead costs are divided among the apartments, taking into account the respective rental areas.

DEFINITION

Working capital = Current assets − Current liabilities

First, you determine the *current assets*. Put simply, the assets that are available within a relatively short term. These include, of course, the money on bank accounts and in cash registers, but also stocks, sellable stocks, and receivables.

To calculate the *working capital*, you simply subtract the *current liabilities* from the currently available assets. The current liabilities include all debts that must or will be cleared within 1 year. In the best case, an amount that is considerably above zero remains.

Return on Investment

When you make an investment, for instance, when you buy machinery, you want to know how cost-effective this is for the capital invested.

DEFINITION

$$\text{Return on Investment (ROI)} = \frac{\text{Earning}}{\text{Capital employed}}$$

Let's assume that your *capital employed* is $10 and you use it to generate an *earning* $3 after a specific period of time, then the *Return on Investment* (ROI) is 0.3. So each dollar you invest becomes $1.30. According to this, it is good if the ROI is greater than 0.

In this context, it is insignificant if you make such minor investments or investments of billions or consider the entire enterprise itself as an investment.

2.4 ANALYSIS METHODS

The financial key figures presented in the previous section are all snapshots without any exceptions, which usually refer to a single scenario, for example, to a specific quantity produced.

Techniques for Decision-Making

Reality, however, constantly provides enterprises with a whole series of options. But which one is the best? Business management offers some well-known techniques for this decision-making in order to make different scenarios assessable.

2.4.1 **Break-Even Analysis**

Let's assume that an enterprise must decide to run production in the United States or abroad. The various national markets have different price and cost structures. In other words, the revenues to be obtained, on the one hand, and the production costs, on the other hand, differ in the markets at choice (Figure 2.10). Which constellation is necessary so that the enterprise chooses the United States?

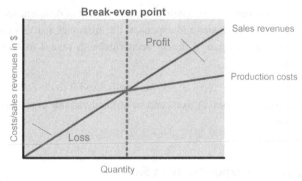

■ **FIGURE 2.10** Break-Even Point

Break-Even Point

Very simply: It stays if it is more likely to gain profit in the United States than abroad with the same quantity.[7] The quantity where the profit zone begins is referred to as *break-even point*.

Both the gradient and the origin of the straight line typically run differently. While the *sales revenues* start at the point of origin, *production costs* already arise, even if not a single unit has been produced yet. Moreover, the sales revenues have a stronger increase than the costs, so that the two straight lines eventually meet at the break-even point. You can calculate this point using the following formula:

---

[7]We beg your pardon: This decision is not that easy, of course. This strong simplification only serves for clarification and not to reinforce stereotypes.

DEFINITION

$$\text{Break-even point} = \frac{\text{Fixed costs}}{\text{Sales price} - \text{Variable costs per unit}}$$

If the production costs were identical in both countries, then the enterprise would stay in the country that has a stronger sales revenue line (in other words, the country where higher prices can be reached with identical costs). You can go through the other possible scenarios yourself.

2.4.2 **Crossover Analysis**

While the break-even analysis enables the assessment of different scenarios with regard to sales revenues and expenses, the crossover analysis uses the same principle to compare different scenarios with regard to fixed and variable costs.

Remember your car? In Section 2.3, we briefly used it to describe the difference between fixed costs (taxes, and so on) and variable costs (costs for gas, and so on).

Porsche is More Expensive than Smart

If you only differentiate by costs and think about whether you want to drive Porsche Cayenne or Smart, then you don't need a crossover analysis. Compared with Smart, Porsche is clearly superior, both with regard to fixed costs and variable costs.

If you want to decide between a diesel-driven and a gasoline-driven car for the same car type, then it's worth calculating the crossover point (Figure 2.11).

Diesel versus Gas

In Figure 2.11, scenario 2 presents the diesel car. Due to higher acquisition costs, the line starts further up on the y-axis, and its lower gas costs cause a lower increase of the line. For the gasoline-driven car, the line starts further down, due to lower acquisition costs, and increases greater as a result of higher gas prices. The two lines intersect at the crossover point.

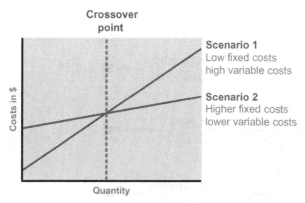

Crossover
point

Scenario 1
Low fixed costs
high variable costs

Scenario 2
Higher fixed costs
lower variable costs

Costs in $

Quantity

■ **FIGURE 2.11** *Crossover Point*

In business management, the horizontal axis usually involves quantities. In this example, however, we don't use the quantity, but the annual mileage.[8]

2.4.3 **Decision Trees**

Sometimes you simply lose track if you have too many options. Then it is useful if you can visualize the various scenarios to be assessed in a *decision tree* (Figure 2.12).

Study or Earn Money?

The decision tree is somewhat similar to life: You get to a fork in the path and must decide whether to turn left or right (study or earn money?). Then you get to another fork which may lead to more directions (three different job offers). Every fork is connected with probabilities of occurrence. At the end, you reach the leaves, and you can assess each path by considering the probabilities.

2.4.4 **Scheduling and Resource Planning**

Scheduling and resource planning enables you to estimate whether projects can be completed within the timeframe required and whether the required resources are actually available.

One technique available in this context is the network plan where a project is split into individual tasks (A, B, C...), which are then put into sequences (Figure 2.13). Some tasks are independent of each other and can be performed simultaneously. For each task you can specify the earliest and latest

---

[8]Unless you are a car dealer.

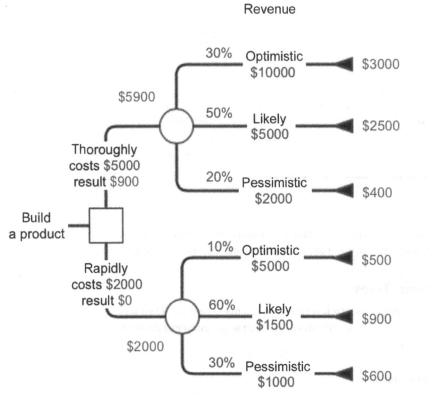

■ FIGURE 2.12 Decision Tree

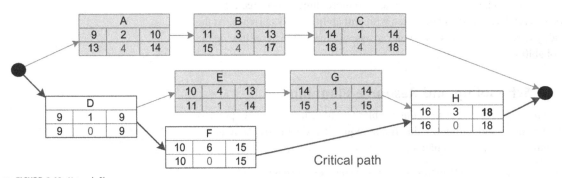

■ FIGURE 2.13 Network Plan

start time, their minimum runtime, and the earliest and latest stop time. This information can be used to determine the tasks that have a time buffer and which tasks are on the *critical path*. If there are any delays on this critical path, this results in delays in the overall project.

2.5 **SAMPLE QUESTIONS**

Here you can test your knowledge on the *Basic Principles of Business Management* topic. Have fun!

You can find the correct answers in Section 8.4, Table A.1.

1. Which of the following items describe the project management process?
   (a) Negotiate, estimate, budget, report
   (b) Initiation, planning, executing, controlling, closing
   (c) Cost, time, quality, scope
   (d) Plan, do, act, fix
2. According to the book "MBA in a day": which definition describes the marketing process?
   (a) Marketing is a process which ensures that brochures and the like are being manufactured in high quality and which arranges the stand at a trade fair.
   (b) Marketing is a synonym for distribution. Therefore its goal is to bring new products and services to the market and sell them with the highest possible price.
   (c) Marketing is a social and managerial process by which individuals and groups obtain what they need and want through creating, offering, and exchanging products of value with others.
   (d) Marketing is the systematization of generating leads (by taking out adverts on different media channels), evaluating each lead and then routing them to the sales department.
3. Which are elements of an effective marketing strategy?
   (a) Initiation, planning, executing, controlling, closing
   (b) Market segmentation, strategy development, market research, pricing, placement, and value chain
   (c) Inbound logistics, outbound logistics, marketing and sales, service
   (d) Potential competitors, suppliers, consumers, substitute products, and rivalry among competitors
4. What is a value chain?
   (a) It includes inbound logistics, operations, outbound logistics, marketing and sales, service, firm infrastructure, human resources management, and technology.
   (b) It creates value to the market by considering demographic, technological, economic, and political factors.
   (c) It is a chain of actions that measure the increasing value of an economic good being manufactured.
   (d) The value chain describes the performance of a set of company shares. Common examples of value chains are Dow Jones and DAX.

5. What is the break-even point?
   (a) A special item on a Balanced Score Card (BSC)
   (b) The point at which production costs are equal to the sales revenues
   (c) The point at which a company becomes insolvent
   (d) The point at which variable costs overtakes the overhead costs
6. Which business function is a support function?
   (a) Sales
   (b) Human resources
   (c) Accounting
   (d) Project management
7. Which statement about the working capital is correct?
   (a) It is the company's current assets that are bearing interest.
   (b) It is the company's liabilities divided by its current assets.
   (c) It is the limit of the amount that can be withdrawn at a cash point within 1 day.
   (d) It describes the company's ability to pay its current obligations.
8. Which are the main management skills?
   (a) Communication, research, and pricing
   (b) Planning, executing, and closing
   (c) Goal-setting, planning, and controlling
   (d) Analyzing, calculating, and facility managing
9. What is the main goal of the business function "Finance"?
   (a) To manage financial instruments in order to keep the competitors breathless
   (b) To ensure that the company has enough money it needs to keep the business running
   (c) To be informed where the money comes from and where it goes to
   (d) To decide on expenses, be responsible for mismanagement and collect bonuses

Chapter 3

Basic Principles of Business Processes

Imagination is more important than knowledge.

Albert Einstein

Mainly independent of concrete standards such as the BPMN, this chapter describes the general basic principles of business processes.

3.1 WHAT IS A BUSINESS PROCESS?

OCEB2 REFERENCE

Jon Siegel, OMG's OCEB2 Certification Program, What is the Definition of Business Process? [30].

Question

The general question of what a business process is cannot be answered easily because there is no uniform definition. But, as a matter of course, a certification program on business process management must ask this question. And it is important to have a uniform understanding of the meaning of the term, *business process*, not only in the certification program, but also in real life. Almost all subsequent concepts are based on it. And if the basis is fragile, many things can go wrong.

Answer: Real Life

But how do we get out of this dilemma? In real life, you should communicate your understanding of a business process and align it with your project

OCEB 2 Certification Guide. http://dx.doi.org/10.1016/B978-0-12-805352-2.00003-0

team members and other contact persons. It is not important how you define the business process, but that all persons involved use the same definition.

Answer: OCEB2

The certification program OCEB2 has not decided on any definition of an author or standard, but created its own paper that describes typical characteristics of a business process and addresses the variety of definitions [30]. This much better reflects the goal of OCEB2, to certify business process management knowledge because this variety is part of real life.

Characteristics of business processes that you can find in many definitions include:

- They involve several actions, steps, and activities.
- They usually involve various organizational units (departments, enterprises, etc.).
- They are targeted.
- They basically describe an action, decision, and cooperation.
- The result represents a value for an (internal or external) customer.

Other critical characteristics of business processes can be as follows:

- They describe how the enterprise (or other organizational unit) operates.
- Actions can be assigned to organizational units or roles.
- The more *branches* a business processes has, the more complex it is.

Definitions of Authors

One definition is provided by the authors Geary A. Rummler and Alan P. Brache [29], who describe the business process as a series of steps designed to produce a product or service. If the result is directly of benefit for the customer, it is a primary process, otherwise it is a supporting process. Martyn Ould defines business processes as a coherent set of activities carried out by a collaborating group to achieve a goal [27]. The authors, Howard Smith and Peter Fingar, define the business process in a similar way and supplement characteristics [34]. According to this definition, a business process is complex, distributed, and long-running.

Definitions in Standards

The definition of business process in standards is similar to the definitions of authors. The glossary of *Workflow Management Coalition* (WfMC) describes the business process as a set of one or more linked procedures or activities which collectively realize a business objective or policy goal, normally within the context of an organizational structure defining functional roles and relationships [8]. OMG also has its own opinion on the business process. In the *Business Motivation Model* standard (BMM), the business process is defined as an unit that implements strategies and tactics so that the enterprise achieves its goals [2].

Similarities and Differences

You possibly know many more definitions. But all of these definitions are essentially very similar. They describe how an enterprise works. The difference is in the limiting characteristics and the business process's level of detail. For example, the definition of BMM is very general and permits almost all business workflows as a business process. Geary A. Rummler and Alan P. Brache request a customer-related result, and Howard Smith and Peter Fingar characterize business processes as long-running. According to some definitions, a business process has a start and an end. According to other definitions, continuous activities, such as risk management, are business processes as well. For real life and for the certification, it is important to know this wide range of definitions.

3.2 CHARACTERISTICS OF A BUSINESS PROCESS

OCEB2 REFERENCE

James F. Chang, Business Process Management Systems [6]; Howard Smith und Peter Fingar, Business Process Management: The Third Wave [34]; Laury Verner, The Challenge of Process Discovery [37].

Complexity

Business processes are complex according to Howard Smith and Peter Fingar [34]. The characteristic of complexity is often used if things get complicated. There are innumerous discussions on the difference between complex and complicated. If you're interested in this topic, simply browse the Internet. There are a vast number of different opinions on this topic. We'll only examine which characteristic makes a business process complex. Imagine the process operation in the form of a flowchart, for instance, in BPMN as shown in Figure 3.1.

Major Doesn't Mean Complex

You can see that it is not the number of steps that makes a process complex. Major, comprehensive processes can be very simple. The number of

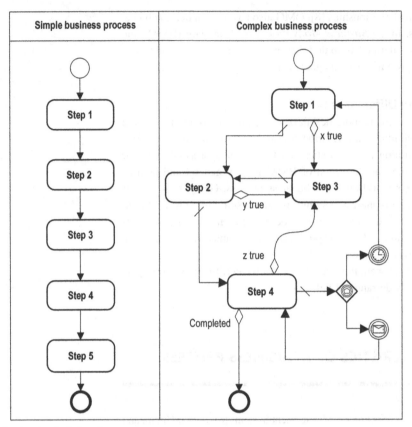

■ **FIGURE 3.1** Simple versus Complex Business Process

branches is decisive, which make the process complex and unclear for the persons involved. This particularly applies if the business process is not described.

Flexibility as a Success Factor

A very important, but not inherent, characteristic of a business process is the ability to be changed easily. Enterprises are subject to constant changes in the market and must adapt to those in a flexible way if they want to be successful in the long term. For example, *SpeedyCar* only had call centers and some subsidiaries as points of contact for its customers for many years. Market conditions have forced the enterprise to provide its services also via the Internet since the beginning of 2000. Currently, changes must be made due to the *mobile computing* trend. Customers surf the web anywhere and anytime via their cell phones and similar devices. This results in changed, and even completely new, business processes.

Active Business Process Management

To ensure that an enterprise can successfully respond to changes, it must actively run a business process management. In dynamic markets, a process-focused organization proves itself in contrast to a function-focused organization, which focuses on departments like finance, customer service, human resources, and so on (Section 4.2). A critical aspect is that business processes are considered and handled as *assets* within the enterprise (see also Section 4.1).

Role

Human beings are a central element in the world of processes. They invent processes, execute them, and they are made for them. But processes are not oriented toward individuals, but toward roles, in other words, there is no process that describes the tasks of Tim Weilkiens or Christa Preisendanz. But there are processes describing how Tim in the role of an author of this book cooperates with Christa as the editor. If these roles are assigned to other concrete persons, they follow the same process. The roles work together to fulfill the tasks. The activities cannot be viewed separately by roles. It is the interaction that provides added value.

Role descriptions exist at different abstraction levels and they can represent a different number of possible concrete persons. The role of the managing director at *SpeedyCar* stands for a concrete person (Mr. Speedy). The role of the call center agent is assumed by several persons and the role of the customer (hopefully) by a great many people. The role of the applicant has an abstract character, that is, the role can be assumed by another role, for instance, the customer, which is then occupied by a concrete person.

Process Steps

Another central element of a process involves the process steps, that is, the activities executed by the roles. Besides the sequence of steps, which is determined by the process, business rules must also be adhered to when they are executed. These include, for example, organizational policies and standards. Section 7.1 describes the meaning of these terms.

Process Topology

The explicit process is determined by its topology, that is, by the steps and their interrelations. Flowcharts—created using BPMN, for example

(Chapter 6)—visualize this topology. So, one form of process discovery might be to work out the upstream or downstream step of an activity to compile the business process successively. Figure 3.2 shows the business process, *invoice monthly services*, as a flowchart in BPMN. Chapter 6 provides some charts that also describe the topic of monthly statements. A good BPMN reading exercise: What are the differences?

Horizontal versus Vertical

The flowchart shows the process topology in the horizontal level. Vertically, you can view the process hierarchy, which shows that processes can be part of a superordinate process. Process steps can be described in detail by processes until you come across activities or actions that can no longer be broken down to the lowest level. Note that the distinction between horizontal and vertical structures also exists for organization units and business processes, where they consider another aspect, however (Section 4.2).

For processes, the main focus is often on flowcharts. But there's additional information available for a business process:

- *Process owner*
- Goals of the business process
- The customer who benefits from the business process
- The stakeholders who can provide important information on the process
- A brief description of the process

The activities—the elementary steps of a process—also have characteristics such as

- Executing role ("work unit")
- Necessary resources
- Data that is required or generated
- Duration
- Business rules that must be taken into account
- A brief description of the activity

Process Goal

As already determined in Section 3.1, a business process usually is not a random sequence of activities, but a sequence that pursues one or more goals. The term *goal* is a general word whose meaning we want to outline briefly here to avoid misunderstandings. A goal is a targeted, desirable state. In our context, we consider not only the final goals, but also goals—that is, states—which can also be achieved in the course of the business process. The goal can describe a unique state or a *steady-state goal*, for example, "the complaint rate must be below 0.5% of all bookings."

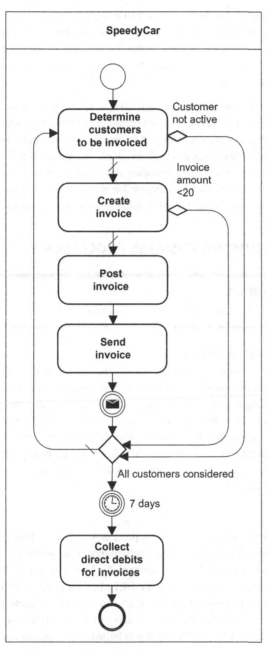

■ **FIGURE 3.2** Process Topology in BPMN

At least one goal should be assigned to every business process. Start and intermediate states can also be described. It thus becomes apparent how the business processes change the states in the course of time, for example, from the state of "customer requests a service" to the state and goal of "customer is satisfied."

This information on processes and activities seems to be easy and only needs to be written down. In real life, however, this is different. Frequently, knowledge only exists implicitly within the organizations and must be detected first. Section 3.3 discusses this topic in detail. The initial recording of business processes is also a manifestation that creates change requirements because the documentation reveals possible weaknesses of the business process. It is therefore also important to distinguish actual and target processes.

3.3 DISCOVERING BUSINESS PROCESSES

OCEB2 REFERENCE

Laury Verner, The Challenge of Process Discovery [37].

From Implicit to Explicit

Do you have a book in your desk drawer that describes the business processes of your organization? Probably not, and you presumably don't have a corresponding model or document in your IT department, either. But business processes definitely exist—frequently only as implicit, distributed knowledge within the organization. This becomes particularly apparent when persons take their knowledge when they leave the enterprise. The goal of process discovery is to detect implicit knowledge about actual processes and make it explicit.

Basis

The explicit knowledge on business processes forms the basis of process improvements. You cannot effectively improve or automate processes which you don't know. The supporters of *Business Process Reengineering* (BPR) object to this statement (Section 4.1). In their opinion, the documentation of actual processes takes too long and is too incomplete to provide valuable results. It would be more effective to redevelop the business process from scratch. In the 1990s, BPR was hailed as a revolutionary approach and an important driver of the BPM discipline; Currently, it is viewed more critically.

Business Process Analysis

The purpose of *Business Process Analysis* (BPA) is to provide explicit process knowledge. It serves to discover weaknesses and enables actual/target comparisons. In his article on process discovery, Laury Verner lists typical examples that require BPA [37]:

- Diagnosing the root cause for a known process problem, such as finding out why the warranty process takes so long
- Finding unknown weaknesses and bottlenecks in existing processes
- Understanding the interrelations and integration of hundreds of data and documents
- Creating standard processes for supply chain interactions, for instance, using SCOR (Section 7.2.2)
- Converging multiple parallel processes, performed by different departments, into a single enterprise-wide standard process
- Preparing for measure implementation, specifically to perform an analysis of the new measures on existing processes, for instance, the application of new business rules
- Generating functional requirements on an IT system
- Designing the business logic of a process that will be automated using commercial *Business Process Management Suite* product (BPMS)

BPA Process

Discovering and documenting are the first steps in the explicit consideration of the business process. This is followed by the analysis of the actual process; the process design of a new target process which erases the weaknesses of the actual process; the development of the target process; the introduction, implementation, and finally, the maintenance of the current process (Figure 3.3).

Roles

As described previously, a process also includes roles that execute the process steps. There are three roles involved in the process discovery:

- The sponsor who sets up the BPA project assumes responsibility for it and specifies goals.
- The *Subject Matter Experts* (SME) who provide the process content. They frequently come from the management level.
- The analysts who control and implement the methodologies of BPA.

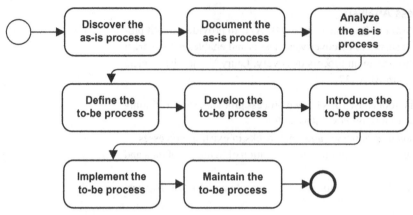

■ **FIGURE 3.3** Process of BPA as a BPMN Diagram

Approach
Laury Verner differentiates three different ways to approach process discovery [37]:

Centralized
Centralized versus distributed approach—In the centralized methodology, the analyst assembles multiple SME's together for a series of workshop sessions. This merging of cumulative expert knowledge can lead to positive synergy effects. Predominate SMEs, however, can enforce their opinion toward less dominant persons and thus, distort the results. Organization-wise, however, this approach proves difficult, because bringing all SMEs together at the same time, particularly if they come from the enterprise's management, is a difficult task.

Distributed
The distributed approach is more democratic because the SMEs are interviewed separately by the analyst and consequently, all opinions can be handled equally. It is the analyst's task to bring all process fragments together and solve inconsistencies. A subsequent review conducted by the previously interviewed persons often reveals whether all findings have been recorded correctly and all inconsistencies have been removed.

Top-Down
Top-down versus bottom-up approach—The top-down approach is the classic method. The analyst starts with an enterprise-wide process with a low level of detail, for instance, car rental. He identifies the steps of the

process and describes each of these steps with a more detailed process, and so on. This approach ensures that the context initially selected is kept. The disadvantage is that process steps which do not fit in the specified hierarchy easily remain undiscovered.

Bottom-Up

The bottom-up approach starts with the detailed activities. The SMEs report directly about their work steps. This results in a high level of detail. This advantage is a disadvantage at the same time. The analyst can easily get lost in trivial details. His challenge is to put the various pieces of information in the right context to illustrate the process hierarchy, and to determine whether the processes have been identified completely in compliance with the set goal.

Structured

Structured versus free form approach—In the structured approach, the SMEs answer predefined questions from the analysts. Ideally, this takes place interactively, but it can also be implemented separately, using questionnaires. The structured approaches lead to consistent results. But they can also be incomplete if the contents do not comply with the predefined questions.

Free Form

In the free form approach, the SME reports to the analyst without predefined specifications. The random degrees of freedom allow for the exchange of any information. It is the analyst's task to convert this unstructured information into a structured form.

Orthogonal Approaches

The tree approaches are not mutually exclusive, but are orthogonal. You can take the centralized, top-down, and structured approach or centralized, bottom-up, and free form, and so on. In the case of a newly conducted process analysis of the entire enterprise, Laury Verner suggests to first gain a rough overview of the process structure in a top-down approach. Details can then be supplemented bottom-up to check them for completeness and to remove inconsistencies in a third step (usually using a tool). Subject Matter Experts and the most critical stakeholders can then do a review to obtain a result that is accepted by the enterprise.

3.4 **DEGREES OF ABSTRACTION OF PROCESS DESCRIPTIONS**

OCEB2 REFERENCE

Bruce Silver, Three Levels of Process Modeling with BPMN [32]; BPMN specification [4].

You can model business processes in three distinct levels [32]:

1. *Descriptive modeling*
2. *Analytical modeling*
3. *Executable modeling*

Descriptive

The descriptive level maps business processes in a high level of detail. It provides an overview of the process—usually in the best case—and of the organization units and roles involved. Simple diagrams, for instance, using BPMN, or text descriptions can be used for this purpose. The description's goal is to communicate business processes across organization units, for example, to the upper management.

Analytical

The analytic process description features a considerably higher level of detail. Not only the best case, but also the variants and exceptions of the business process are described here. The analyst must have advanced skills in modeling, for instance, *workflow patterns*, troubleshooting, and handling of events. The result of analytical modeling can be used to analyze the effectiveness of processes. This is also the level of detail that IT departments require to create an implementation that automates the business process completely, or in parts.

Executable

Executable modeling means that the process model itself is executable and can be directly used for automating the business process. This requires a very high level of detail and presents a corresponding challenge to the modeler. BPMN supports the creation of executable models, for example. In real life, however, the modeling tools often differ from the standard and use tool-specific concepts to enable feasibility.

The target group of a business process description is very heterogeneous. Therefore, it is not sufficient to just distinguish the form of presentation.

Another view and distinction originates directly from the BPMN specification [4]: private, public, and collaborative business processes. Naturally, this differentiation refers to BPMN. However, this view can also be generalized and transferred to other description forms.

Private Business Process

Most business processes fall into the category of *private business processes*. They are representations of internal flows that are specific for the organization. Figure 3.4 shows the private business process, *book car*.

Public Business Process

Public business processes describe the interaction between a private business process and one or more parties involved. Only those process steps that are involved in the interaction of the private process are illustrated. The process steps of the interaction partners are not described. Figure 3.5 shows the interactions of the private process from Figure 3.4, with the group able to book a car of a partner in another city. Public business processes are also referred to as abstract business processes.

Collaborative Business Process

A *collaborative process* shows an interaction, just like the public business processes. However, you can now also include the detailed process steps of the parties involved and the exact sequence of information exchange. Figure 3.6 shows the business process of car booking as a collaborative model.

Mixing Aspects

The distinction between private, public, and collaborative business processes is independent of the previously described abstractions of descriptive, analytical, and executable modeling. For example, you can model private business processes as analytical, or describe public business processes.

Besides the level of detail of a process diagram, you can also distinguish between the actual and target processes. Actual processes describe the actual business process. They are usually described to make the enterprise's implicit process knowledge transparent and to serve as the basis for optimizations. Target processes describe the target condition of a business process after an analysis and optimization was made, for example. Target processes are used if they involve new business processes that must be integrated with the existing organization.

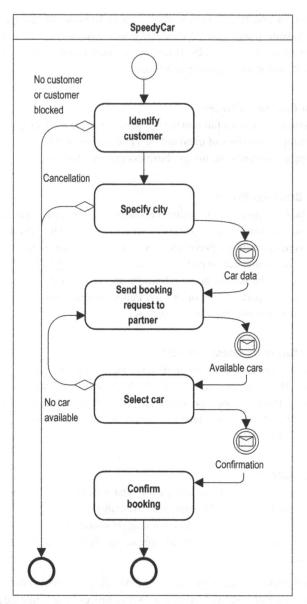

■ **FIGURE 3.4** Private Business Process

To design business process models meaningfully for others, Ould [27] suggests pursuing the following modeling principles:

- If there are abstraction levels, they should follow a purpose.
- Reality is chaotic.

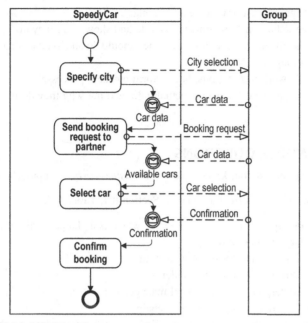

■ **FIGURE 3.5** Public Business Process

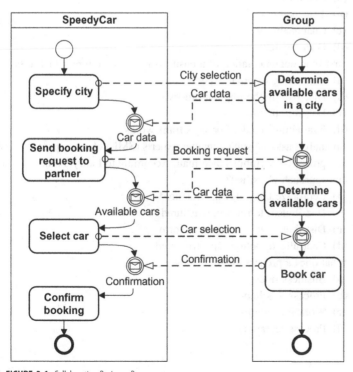

■ **FIGURE 3.6** Collaborative Business Process

- A diagram must have a clear meaning.
- Process diagrams are aimed at people and show what they do.
- On the one hand, they show what they should do and, on the other hand, what they actually do.
- People work in functions, but perform business processes.
- It is about what the people actually do, and not why they do it.

3.5 **SAMPLE QUESTIONS**

Here you can test your knowledge on the *business process* topic. Have fun!

You can find the correct answers in Section 8.4, Table A.2.

1. According to Rummler and Brache, which is a characteristic of a primary business process?
   (a) Direct value for external customers
   (b) Direct value for stakeholder
   (c) Under control of top-level management
   (d) Covers first part of a value chain
2. What is a stable and important ability of a business process?
   (a) Complexity
   (b) Transparency
   (c) Changeability
   (d) Documented
3. First time documentation of a business process requires which task?
   (a) Consulting external experts
   (b) Discovering the implicit process
   (c) Defining the process
   (d) Evaluating standard process frameworks
4. An analyst asks all subject matter experts (SME) of a company to send him process descriptions by e-mail. According to Laury Verner, how is this approach classified?
   (a) Centralized, top-down, structured
   (b) Distributed, top-down, structured
   (c) Distributed, bottom-up, free form
   (d) Centralized, bottom-up, structured
5. What does a process diagram show?
   (a) Business rules
   (b) Process topology
   (c) Work procedures
   (d) Process hierarchy

6. Which statement describes a process goal?
   (a) After approval of the request for participation, the company sends the acknowledgement and customer card to the customer.
   (b) The customer must pay the invoices within 3 weeks.
   (c) After approval of the request for participation, the candidate becomes an activated customer of the car rental company.
   (d) A customer with no transactions within the last 6 months will be deactivated.
7. What is a typical area of application for a BPA?
   (a) To establish a new business
   (b) To detect process bottlenecks
   (c) To define process roles
   (d) To analyze the market
8. Which level of process modeling is used to provide requirements for an IT implementation of a business process?
   (a) Descriptive modeling
   (b) Software modeling
   (c) Executable modeling
   (d) Analytical modeling

Chapter 4

Basic Principles of Business Process Management

Continuous improvement is better than delayed perfection.

Mark Twain

Just like in Chapter 3, this chapter now deals with general basic principles apart from concrete standards.

4.1 WHAT IS BUSINESS PROCESS MANAGEMENT?

OCEB2 REFERENCE

James F. Chang, Business Process Management Systems [6].

Origin

When you search for the origins of *Business Process Management* (BPM), you ultimately end up with Adam Smith and his work, *The Wealth of Nations*, written in 1776 [33]. He determined that productivity can be increased considerably by division of labor and specialization. This requires the definition of roles, associated tasks, and a description of how they collaborate. This takes us to explicit business processes which should be controlled by management. The functional units are still the status quo in many enterprises, even today. However, the focus is instead on isolated optimization of individual process steps and not on the course of the entire process. Consequently, it is not optimal all the time and leads to increased costs and

OCEB 2 Certification Guide. http://dx.doi.org/10.1016/B978-0-12-805352-2.00004-2

undesirable results. However, viewing the process flow—from the start to the end—is decisive. An up-to-date view of the topic is that it's the business process management's task to define and implement processes, support performance measurements based on predefined process goals, and optimize processes. It's important to know the process owner when you define and monitor the processes, so that processes can be oriented towards the customers and run optimally.

To find the roots of today's BPM, you typically don't go back to Adam Smith, but you usually end up with *Total Quality Management* (TQM) and *Business Process Reengineering* (BPR) from the 1980s and 1990s.

TQM

The initial ideas on TQM were developed by William Edwards Deming, Joseph Juran, and Kaoru Ishikawa in the 1940s. But it was not until the 1980s that the high market pressure, particularly coming from Japanese enterprises, lead to a widespread use of TQM.

Definition

It is difficult to define TQM. One of the originators—William Edwards Deming—even said that TQM was only a buzzword, and that he never used the term and it didn't have any meaning [12]. The fact that he rejects the term TQM doesn't mean, of course, that he also rejects the concepts of TQM. J. Richard Hackmann and Ruth Wageman provided a sound and acknowledged description of these concepts [21]: The purpose of an organization is to sustain itself so that it can contribute to the stability of the community, provide goods and services to customers and provide an environment for organization members to grow. TQM is also a technique to run continuous quality improvement projects on a regular basis. The principles of TQM include the following:

- *Management by process* because quality problems often arise there.
- Analysis of variability because uncontrolled variances are the main cause for quality problems.
- Management by fact because quality improvement projects should work on a systematic data basis about the processes.
- Quality improvement is a never-ending process.

The specific techniques of TQM involve:

- Determine customer requirements
- Establish supplier relationships on a partnership basis
- Set up cross-functional teams for quality improvement

The benefits of TQM and particularly, process focusing, include faster response to market changes and cross-functional communication and collaboration within the enterprise. On the downside, however, some functional capabilities must be doubled because they occur in multiple processes. In addition, if a functional organization structure is maintained during *management by process*, that is, if it is converted to a matrix organization, the organization's complexity increases.

BPR

In the 1990s, the attention shifted from TQM to *Business Process Reengineering* (BPR). This shift was initiated by an article by Thomas Davenport and James R. Short [11], and an article by Michael Hammer [23].

The first article suggests a five-step methodology for achieving process redesign (Figure 4.1). Two assumptions form the basis of this process:

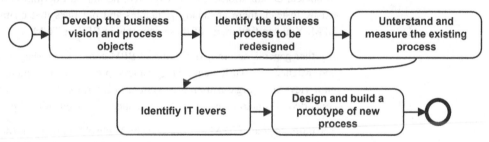

■ **FIGURE 4.1** Process Improvement According to Davenport

- IT is a *key enabler* of BPM.
- Process improvement is oriented toward goals and not toward fixing local bottlenecks and other process weaknesses.

Radical Approach

The second article by Michael Hammer was published roughly at the same time. He, as well, considers IT as a key enabler, but his approach is considerably more radical. Instead of improving existing processes, he propagates to develop them completely from scratch.

Leaps Instead of Steps

The goal is to achieve huge progress with regard to cost reduction and quality improvement and not small, incremental steps that take too long overall and thus can existentially jeopardize the enterprise.

In the new development, everything is aligned with the processes. They, and not the individual tasks, take center stage. Consequently, this leads to a process-focused organization (Section 4.2).

Hammer and Champy

The approach of BPR is described comprehensively in the book, *Reengineering the Corporation: A Manifestation for Business Revolution*, written by Michael Hammer and James Champy [24].

BPM

In the mid-1990s—particularly due to TQM and BPR—business process management was labeled as an explicit discipline for the first time. It is a management approach that creates the environment necessary to implement improvement methodologies, such as Six Sigma (Chapter 7, Section "Six Sigma"), TQM, or BPR. The close proximity of these methodologies leads to unclear delimitations, and, as expected, no uniform definition of BPM exists. Instead, there are many principles and practices that characterize BPM. You can find many of these concepts in BPR or TQM.

A rather general, common definition of BPM comes from Mary J. Benner and Michael L. Tushmann [1]: Business process management, based on a view of an organization as a system of interlinked process, involves concerted efforts to map, improve, and adhere to organizational processes.

The ultimate goal of BPM was specified by Michael Hammer, who defines it as the improvement of products and services using structured service optimization based on systematic design and management of business processes. Admittedly, this is still very vague and difficult to realize. James F. Chang defines the term BPM in more detail and described four principles and eight tools of BPM for this purpose [6].

Processes Are Assets

Principle 1—Business processes are central *assets* of the organization to meet customer requirements. It is these assets that create values for the customer, and not an individual person or organization unit. The sales and marketing departments of *SpeedyCar*, for example, cannot render any values for the customers without car service and system development. Therefore, business processes are considered as assets which are directly invested in.

Processes Should Be Managed

Principle 2—As assets, business processes must be managed explicitly. This includes the measuring, monitoring, controlling, and analyzing of business processes, which results in consistent outcomes for the customer and forms the basis for process improvements.

Processes Should Be Continuously Improved

Principle 3—Business processes must be improved continuously. It is not a one-time task to implement improvements but a continuous, never-ending task.

IT Is an Essential Enabler

Principle 4—The use of information technology is essential for the success of BPM. IT delivers information that is required to manage business processes.

Practices

The principles are guidelines that lead the way for BPM. The eight practices provide concrete specifications of the tasks to be performed.

Organization Structure

Practice 1—Establish process-focused organization structures.

Process Owner

Practice 2—Nominate *process owners*. They are responsible for the success of their processes. For this purpose, they must reconcile with the functional units that are affected by the process. *SpeedyCar*'s process owner that is responsible for the *car rental* process must collaborate with the managers of the functional units, call center, car service, customer support, and accounting, so that his process runs optimally.

Bottom-Up Support

Practice 3—The upper management must support and promote BPM. The process is improved from bottom to top (bottom-up approach).

IT

Practice 4—Establish IT systems to monitor, control, analyze, and improve business processes. IT plays a critical role in the world of business processes. In the 1990s, IT was entitled as a *key enabler* of process management within the scope of the BPR movement. As a result, IT has moved into the limelight. For example, the revenue of SAP—a provider of *Enterprise Resource Planning* (ERP) systems—has increased from €255 million in 1990 to €7.5 billion in 2001 [6].

Such systems cannot be installed and used easily, but require a tedious adaptation. For this purpose, IT experts must closely collaborate with analysts. The convergence of IT and process management theory is a key concept of process management.

A *Business Process Management Suite* (BPMS) is a collection of IT applications that supports and measures the business processes [6]. They support the standardization and linking of business processes. Standardization also involves the integration of data in *back-end systems*.

Business Partners

Practice 5—Collaborate with business partners that are involved in common cross-organizational business processes.

Training and Improvement

Practice 6—Train the employees regularly, and continuously improve the business processes.

Bonus and Awards

Practice 7—Combine process improvement with bonus payments and awards.

Leaps Instead of Steps

Practice 8—Utilize both incremental process improvement measures, such as Six Sigma and more radical approaches, such as BPR.

The question arises as to why an organization should change toward a process-focused organization. The reason can be found in the market that is changing and exerts pressure on the enterprise. Success in the market can no longer be reduced to the simple formula, "faster, better, cheaper":

- Faster—The enterprise that launches a product first is successful.
- Better—The enterprise that launches products with a higher quality is successful.
- Cheaper—The enterprise that can ultimately offer the products at a lower price is success.

Pressure on Enterprises

This formula was valid for a long time. Then, Japanese enterprises, such as Sony and Toyota, emerged that met all three requirements at the same time. This changed market situation has inspired the radical ideas of BPR, among other things. The growing globalization and the associated increase of marketplaces advances the focus on business process management. In their book, Howard Smith and Peter Fingar mention seven trends that illustrate the pressure which enterprises are subject to [34]:

1. *The customer is no longer a king, but a dictator.* Thanks to the Internet, the customers are well-informed and demand what they want.
2. *Mass production makes way for mass customization.* Dell, which offers its customers customized computers, is a good example.

3. *Customers demand holistic solutions.* It is no longer just about a single product, but also about processes. *SpeedyCar* not only offers rental cars. The customers can also call on travel agency services, such as event bookings, or transfers from/to rental offices: A full-service package for all activities that could be related to a drive in the rental car.
4. *The boundaries between industries become blurred.* Because enterprises offer holistic solutions, they also advance in other industry segments. *SpeedyCar*, for example, offers some products of the travel industry, such as transfers and hotel booking services.
5. *Enter partnerships.* When enterprises advance in other industries, they must also enter partnerships, because they cannot meet all requirements by themselves. The successful cooperation with partners requires a sound adaptation of business processes.
6. *Value chains are the measure of competition.* It's no longer just about who has the best product, but who has the best value chains to be able to offer customers a holistic solution.
7. *Change is the only constant.* The rate of changes in the market and the associated pressure on enterprises becomes ever shorter and requires more flexible business processes.

4.2 **PROCESS-FOCUSED ORGANIZATION**

OCEB2 REFERENCE

Daniel J. Madison, *Becoming A Process-Focused Organization* [26].

In most cases, organizations have a function-focused structure. This means that the associated functions are bundled in a unit, for instance, accounting, human resources, or customer service. The business processes are orthogonal to this structure. Alignment along the functions is also referred to as vertical structure, and horizontal structure along the business processes (Figure 4.2). Cross-functional considerations and efficient transfers at the function boundaries are easily forgotten in function-focused organizations. This can lead to inefficient processes despite good functions.

Process-Focused
This is exactly where the focus is in process-focused organizations, and the function structure takes a backseat, or doesn't exist at all. To successfully coordinate the functions involved in the process is one of the challenges of process management. This, however, increases the responsiveness on the market. Concentrating on the horizontal structure may have the

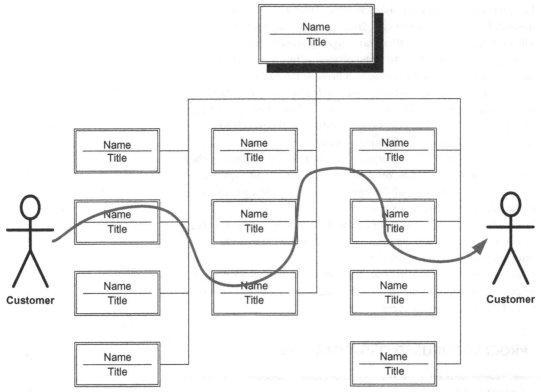

■ **FIGURE 4.2** Function-Focused versus Process-Focused

disadvantage that functional expertise is duplicated, because it is no longer concentrated in the vertical structure.

In his article, *Becoming a Process-Focused Organization* [26], Daniel J. Madison lists several points on culture, concepts, structure, and technique, which a process-focused organization should take into account.

Culture

The organization's values must shift from individual recognition to process excellence. Errors are not considered as errors of individual persons, but as an opportunity to improve processes from the insights gained. As an individual person, I can gain a good reputation if I make valuable contributions to more efficient business processes.

The values of the organization enhance the collaboration of the process teams, and standards of the organizations prevent boundaries and territories from forming in the vertical structure. The process owners and department managers must cooperate closely and respect each other.

The top management must think in processes and not in functions, in other words, they must map projects onto processes, and not onto tasks for the function units.

Concepts

The organization requires a vision and a mission (Chapter 5) to provide the necessary context and focus on the business processes. The strategies must directly relate to the processes. This can be achieved by using *balanced scorecards* (Chapter 7, Section "Balanced Scorecard"). Using process-focused methods like Six Sigma, BPR, or TQM should be promoted.

Structure

Shifting from a function-focused to a process-focused organization also affects the structures of the enterprise. It is necessary to create a *formal governing body* that oversees the organization-wide business processes and sets priorities and provides resources for projects.

The business processes require a process owner, which may represent a new role within the organization. In general, role descriptions should increasingly call for cross-functional abilities to obtain more all-rounders than specialists. The career ladders shift from the vertical to the horizontal structure. The process owner is responsible for the optimal functioning of his process or, if this is not the case, for initiating an optimization measure. He designs the process and implements it in the organization, which would mean in a process organization, that the employees performing the process are subordinated to the process owner. In addition to the process owners who are defined as relatively stable for each process, each project for identifying, optimizing, and implementing a business process requires a sponsor. This sponsor provides the necessary resources, coordinates communication between the process owners involved, and specifies rough objectives and strategies for the processes within his areas of responsibility. To perform and define business processes in detail, you also require *work units* or *lowest level units*, because they know the process in detail and are able to identify weaknesses and develop concrete improvements.

Technology

Of course, technology also plays a special role in a process-focused organization. IT must provide the following for business processes:

- Support by modeling and testing them
- Full or partial automation
- Provision of information, such as key figures

4.3 **BUSINESS PROCESS MANAGEMENT SUITES**

Software plays an ever greater role in process management projects. *Business Process Management Suites* are deployed to perform process redesigns and to manage and automate enterprise processes.

So, IT is considered as a *key enabler* of business process management. In business process management, IT must provide the following:

- Support for definition and optimization
- Implement defined business processes (but not specify the processes), and
- Enable monitoring of operations by providing process data in real time

Business Process Management Suites or Systems (BPMS) integrate existing *back-end systems*, with regard to business process operations and provide them with holistic data for a process instance. They also ensure that all activities are performed by the right resources at the right time. A complete BPMS includes the functions, process modeling, simulation of process designs, and the monitoring of running process instances. During the initial process identification, BPMS supports the validation of processes and identification of incomplete data. If a process must be redesigned, the BPMS helps to illustrate the delta between actual and target processes. Then, simulation can help to identify weak points in a developed process or analyze the suitability of various process variants. Displaying real-time data of implemented process instances supports the monitoring and identification of performance problems during process implementation.

4.4 **DESIGNING EXECUTABLE PROCESS MODELS**

Provided that you also require the technical execution of a process in addition to pure process modeling, that is, the graphical presentation of a process, the process diagram must be transformed into an executable status and transferred to a *process engine*—or *execution engine*—for execution. Some BPMS support both modeling, administration of process models and data, and the execution of processes. In other cases, one tool is used for modeling processes and another one for executing the processes.

The tasks of the *process engine* are as follows:

- Support an executable process design
- Generate executable process instances
- Assign user tasks
- Track and store *execution data*

To design a process diagram in an executable form, the following simplified stages must be completed:

- Classification of process activities into "automated" and "manual" (=user task)
- Re-check of manual activities and possible redesign into automated activities
- Check activities for identical level of granularity (observe 1:1:1 rule: Can the activity be performed without time interruption, by one person, at one place?)
- Adapt the process diagram if required
- Specify attributes of executability (use executable level of BPMN, define process variables, record execution rules, consider BPMS-specific details)

Once the process diagram is enhanced with execution information, the process diagram is exported, transferred to the *process engine*, and executed there. Subsequently, the engine runs the process by calling other required applications, generating user tasks which are displayed in a connected user interface, and monitoring the running process instances in parallel, which can be checked in a monitoring interface.

Digression SOA

Because the topic of service-oriented architecture (SOA) is frequently addressed within the scope of executing process diagrams, also referred to as process automation, we want to mention it briefly here. The goal of a service-oriented architecture is to abstract the mapping of business processes in IT from concrete implementation. In other words, it allows you to describe the necessary processes using services without committing yourself to platforms, programming languages, or other implementation details. The concrete implementation of a business process that was defined using services can still be changed without having to change the definition. Vice versa, a business process can be redefined using the services, for example, to respond to a changed business environment without having to change the implementation as long as you deploy existing services.

Sound IT alone doesn't result in process orientation, but it supports its realization. For this purpose, you require cultural, conceptual, and structural aspects, as described in Section 4.2.

4.5 **SAMPLE QUESTIONS**

Here you can test your knowledge on the *business process management* topic. Have fun!

You can find the correct answers in Section 8.4, Table A.3.

1. Which statement is a business process management principle?
   (a) Business processes should be considered for all enterprise decisions.
   (b) Business processes should be documented.
   (c) Business processes should be automated by a BPMS.
   (d) Business processes should be continuously improved.
2. According to Daniel J. Madison what is a strong value in a process-focused organization?
   (a) Increasing revenue and shareholder values
   (b) Forming vertical structures to horizontal structures
   (c) Coordination within and across process teams
   (d) Automation of business processes
3. What kind of formal governing body is necessary in a process-focused organization?
   (a) A body that oversees the enterprise processes
   (b) A body that controls the department heads and process owners
   (c) A body that specifies IT implementations for process improvements
   (d) A body that provides process models and documentation
4. According to James F. Chang, IT is a key enabler for BPM. For which task is IT important?
   (a) Automating processes
   (b) Implementing Workflow Management Systems
   (c) Providing process information for the management
   (d) Creating process models
5. What is a focus of the process management?
   (a) Shareholders
   (b) Process goals
   (c) Automation
   (d) Quality
6. Which approach is associated with an incremental level of process change?
   (a) BPR
   (b) BPMM
   (c) Adam Smith
   (d) TQM

Business Modeling

People who have a vision should go see a doctor.

Helmut Schmidt

What do you need to create a model of an enterprise? Right. Pen and paper. But which elements do you want to depict?

The *business motivation model* (BMM) provides a structure for defining and developing a business plan by describing which purposes an enterprise pursues with which means. Moreover, it can be used to relate (technical) solutions and developments of the enterprise to business considerations.

It therefore, provides a—if you will—globally uniform comprehension of rather abstract terms, which often totally get mixed up in common speech. You cannot describe the difference between vision and mission straight away, can you? What about strategy and tactic? Neither? Alright, then you should continue reading.

5.1 THE BUSINESS MOTIVATION MODEL

OCEB2 REFERENCE

Business Motivation Model Specification [2]; John Hall, Overview of OMG Business Motivation Model: Core Concepts [22].

The BMM is a standard of OMG and describes, on the one hand, the goals of an enterprise with a superior vision and, on the other hand, the associated implementation strategies and tactics with their superior missions.

No Notation for BMM

There is no standardized *notation*, but only *abstract syntax*. So the BMM only defines structure and properties of the BMM elements such as vision, goals, and so on, and describes their *semantics*.

BMM Area

The top-most areas of BMM are the following (Figure 5.1):

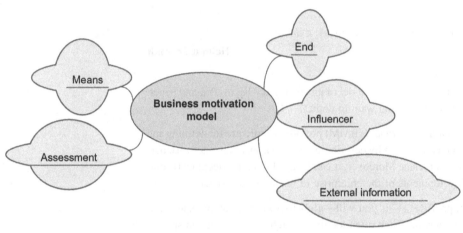

■ **FIGURE 5.1** BMM Main Elements

- *End*—Describes the vision of the enterprise and the goals and objectives derived thereof.
- *Means*—Describes which means the enterprise deploys to meet the enterprise object. This does not refer to employees or money, but to missions, strategies, and tactics.
- *Influencer*—Describes to which influencers the enterprise is exposed, for instance, current market trends, actions of competitors, or internal influencers such as the IT infrastructure.
- *Assessment*—Assesses neutral influencers on goals and means used, for example, that the opening of a rival enterprise nearby poses a threat for the enterprise.
- *External information*—Addresses further important topics of business modeling, which are not part of BMM, but originate from other standards, for example, business processes and organization structures. In this area, BMM defines how these topics are incorporated in the BMM.

5.1.1 **Complete BMM Overview**

Figure 5.2 shows an overview of the topmost elements of BMM.

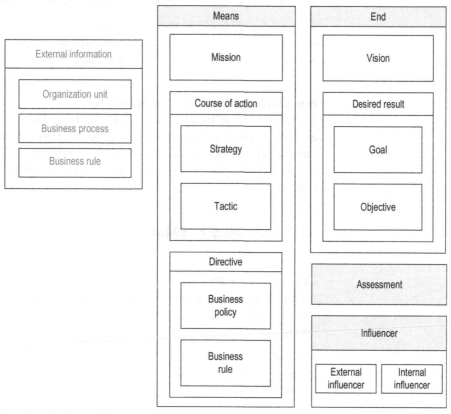

■ **FIGURE 5.2** BMM Area (Complete Overview)

End

The *end* area is divided into *vision* and the *desired results*, which in turn, are subdivided into goals and objectives.

Means

The *means* area is subdivided into *mission*, *course of action*, and *directives*. The course of action is split into *strategy* and *tactic*, and directives into *business policies* and *business rules*.

Influencers

The *influencers* are distinguished by external and internal influencers with reference to the enterprise.

External Information

The external information[1] comprises *organization units, business processes,* and *business rules.* All three information concepts are only referenced here in the BMM and described separately in other standards of OMG:

- *Organization Structure Metamodel* (OSM)[2]
- *Business Process Definition Metamodel* (BPDM)
- *Semantics of Business Vocabulary and Rules* (SBVR)

Non-OMG Standards Are Permitted Too

Incidentally, all of these are also OMG standards whose usage is not expressly mandatory, but helpful at best. These referenced standards are therefore representative for any descriptive form on these topics. You could just as well describe your business processes with eEPC[3] instead of using BPMN.

5.1.2 **Scalability of BMM**

Decomposable Areas

A business model can possibly become very comprehensive. BMM therefore explicitly supports the scalability of very large descriptions in the following three areas:

- *Desired result*
- *Course of action*
- *Business policy*

The elements of these areas can be broken down into subelements using *decomposition.* For example, you can decompose a goal into subordinate goals, which are then included in the superordinate goal.

5.2 **THE ENTERPRISE'S END**

The *end* area describes the purpose of an enterprise, that is, the vision and the desired result in the form of goals and objectives (Figure 5.3). The following sections take a closer look at these elements.

---

[1]Please do not confuse with external influencers.

[2]OSM has never been published. Nevertheless, the definitions and structures of OSM are still a useful source.

[3]eEPC = extended Event-Driven Process Chain.

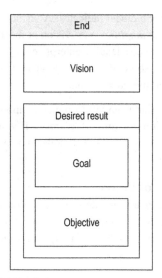

■ **FIGURE 5.3** BMM Area End (Overview)

5.2.1 **Vision**

"I spy with my little eye … a vision." If you apply this typical phrase to an entrepreneur, a vision describes a future image of the enterprise and equally expresses an ultimate, rather impossible, and therefore desirable state, for instance, "We are the leading BPM training enterprise in Europe."

UML for the Metamodel

The metamodel (Figure 5.4) is noted in the UML language, but don't worry: You don't need a certification in UML (*Unified Modeling Language*) for this book. We simply explain what you can read from this image.[4]

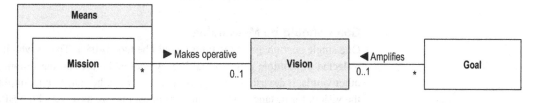

■ **FIGURE 5.4** Vision (Metamodel)

---

[4]If you want to learn more about UML, we recommend—completely without any selfish motives—reading the book "Systems Engineering with SysML/UML" by Tim Weilkiens.

The right-hand side of the model indicates: A vision includes any number[5] of *goals*, and every goal *amplifies* one[6] vision at most. That clearly makes sense: The desire to become a leading enterprise may be a really nice thing. However, you should also be able to derive goals from this desire, which ideally are all based on the same vision.

On the left-hand side (read from left to right) the model states: Every mission can make one vision *operative* at the most. If you read this relation in the opposite direction, it means: Every vision can be made operative by any number of missions.

Different Meanings of Vision

As mentioned previously, a vision describes a future state of the enterprise. But watch out: In everyday language, the word "vision" is also used to describe desirable states outside the enterprise. You certainly know the following:

- *Our vision is a world where everyone can be connected.*

Nokia

- *A PC on every desk in every home.*

Microsoft

These are not visions within the meaning of BMM because the BMM vision is supposed to describe an internal view, in other words, it is supposed to refer to the enterprise and not its environment. This car manufacturer, however, got it right:

Good Example of Vision

Become the world's leading consumer company for automotive products and services.

Ford

5.2.2 **Goals and Objectives**

Goals Should be Measurable

One single neat image of the future would be too abstract. That is why it is reflected in multiple goals in real life. A *goal* elaborates on the vision, in other words, it describes a long-term goal that must be achieved to amplify the vision, for instance, "Our customers attest that we have very high BPM competency." Hmm... shouldn't goals be measurable? Right. Something's missing here (Figure 5.5):

---

[5]Indicated with the multiplicity * (meaning: 0 to any number).
[6]Indicated with the multiplicity 0..1 (meaning: 0–1).

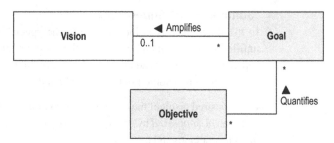

■ **FIGURE 5.5** Goals and Objectives (Metamodel)

Objectives Quantify Goals

BMM also entails objectives in addition to goals. Every goal can have any number of objectives. An *objective* has no direct reference to the vision; instead, it can *quantify* any number of goals—it makes them measurable. Accordingly, an objective is a very concrete, achievable statement with *measure of performance*, for instance, "At the end of next year, 80% of our regular customers evaluate our BPM competency with 9 or better on a scale of 10."

5.2.3 **Desired Result**

Both goals and objectives describe—speaking abstractly—some kind of *desired result*. This term is superordinate of any form of goal or objective, so to speak (Figure 5.6):

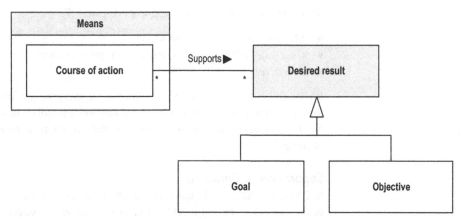

■ **FIGURE 5.6** Goals, Objectives, and Means (Metamodel)

"Some kind of" Superordinate

In the diagram, this is indicated with the special form of the arrow, an unfilled triangle, which points from the concrete term to the more abstract superordinate (to be read as "is some kind of" in the direction of the arrow, that is, "a goal is some kind of desired result").

Every desired result of the enterprise (no matter whether it is a goal or objective) can be *supported* by any number of *courses of action*. Courses of action include strategies and tactics from the *means* area, which we'll discuss in the following.

Remember: The end of a business comprises the vision and the desired results in the form of goals and objectives. All of these elements describe a more or less concrete state which the enterprise wants to achieve sometime in the future. Now you know why this BMM area is called *end*.

5.3 MEANS TO AN END

There's a great quote of Joel Barker, a book author, consultant, and futurist, that emphasizes the significance of the means area:

Passing the Time

> *Vision without action is a dream. Action without vision is simply passing the time. Action with vision is making a positive difference.*
>
> **http://www.joelbarker.com**

In other words: Visions and goals always entail the *means* required to implement them. Means can thus be anything that can be used to achieve goals.

Means mainly consist of three elements (Figure 5.7):

- Missions as the counterpart to vision
- *Courses of action* as the counterpart to desired results
- *Directives*

It should also be noted that the procedures in an enterprise are implemented through business processes to achieve the mission. Moreover, tactics implement strategies, so they are more concrete than the strategic consideration of means.

Separation of Concerns

In BMM, the means of the enterprise are deliberately described independent of the *end*. This concept is referred to as *separation of concerns* and considers that means can change while the goals remain the same. This makes sense.

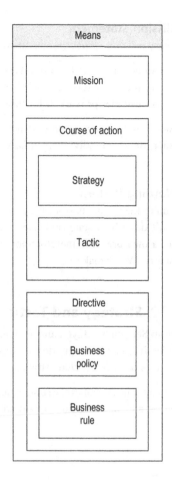

■ **FIGURE 5.7** BMM Area Means (Overview)

5.3.1 **Mission**

A mission describes what an enterprise does to achieve a vision (Figure 5.8):

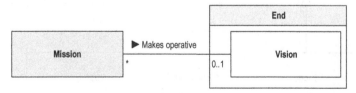

■ **FIGURE 5.8** Mission (Metamodel)

Mission Makes Vision Operative

A mission makes an associated vision *operative* in the first place. There can be any number of missions for a vision. Even if Joel Barker, whom we quoted previously, has something different in mind: BMM allows for a vision without missions and also missions without a vision.

Mission Statement

Every *mission statement* consists of three elements:

- An action in the form of a verb, for instance, offers
- A product or service, for instance, training
- A customer or market, for instance, D.A.CH area[7]

An example for a mission statement would be: "We offer BPM trainings for enterprises and individuals in D.A.CH."

Wording Pattern

Unlike the elements from the *end* area, the elements from the *means* area don't describe a state (indicated with auxiliary verbs like "be" or "can"), but a measure. It is therefore common to word missions according to the pattern "We <make>..."

5.3.2 **Strategy and Tactic**

From Section 5.2.3, you already know that a desired result, that is, a goal or objective, can be supported by any number of *courses of action*. These courses of action include strategies and tactics.

So you can say that every strategy and every tactic is some kind of course of action and, as such, can support any desired results (Figure 5.9).

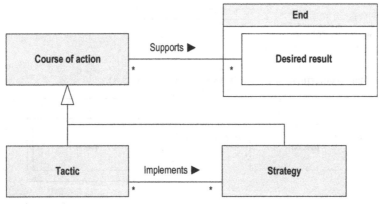

■ **FIGURE 5.9** Course of Action (Metamodel)

---

[7]D.A.CH stands for the market in Germany (D), Austria (A), and Switzerland (CH).

Strategy versus Tactic

What exactly is the difference between strategy and tactic? The model indicates that a *tactic implements* any number of strategies. From this, you can accurately conclude that a tactic already describes a very concrete action, while a strategy is still vague.

Strategies Channel Efforts

A *strategy*, in turn, can be implemented by any number of tactics. BMM considers the strategy as part of the mission's implementation plan to achieve the goals. The fine print says (please remember): *Strategy channels efforts towards goals*. Let this sentence melt in your mouth, it is very interesting. With this sentence, BMM places the strategy from the *means* area on the same level as the goal from the *end* area. In fact, it even requests that a strategy ensures that the "efforts" (this can only be concrete tactics) are aligned with the goals. This also makes sense.

Let's take the following example:

- Goal: "Our customers attest a very high BPM competency."
- Mission: "We offer BPM trainings for enterprises and individuals in D.A.CH."

Strategy Examples

Which means that are suitable for the mission are necessary to achieve this goal? With the following strategies, for example:

- Strategy 1: "We increasingly publish in the BPM area."
- Strategy 2: "We cooperate with an equally renowned Swiss training enterprise in the BPM area."

We don't know for sure whether these strategies really lead to the desired result. But this gives the direction until you decide on other strategies (i.e., change the means).

Tactics for the first strategy could be the following, for example:

- Tactics 2: "Andrea creates webinars and *Web Based Trainings* for the OCEB2 certification."
- Tactics 3: "Tim and Christian write an article on OCEB2 for a professional journal."
- Tactics 4: "Kim offers preparatory courses on OCEB2 certification at the OOP conference."

You can see that this is not as unrealistic as it first seemed.

5.3.3 **Business Principles and Business Rules**

And because our daily working life doesn't have enough trend-setting elements already, there are another two to be considered. The third main element of the *means* area involves the *directive*.

Directives, Business Policies, or Business Rules

While the two courses of action, strategy and tactic, only make statements on what is done, a directive describes how it is done. Every directive can *govern* any number of courses of action and *support* any number of desired results (goals or objectives). A directive is either a *business policy* or a *business rule* (Figure 5.10).

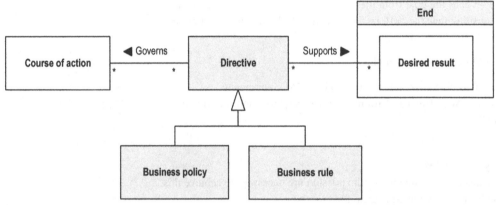

■ **FIGURE 5.10** Directive (Metamodel)

Enforcement Level

BMM provides an *enforcement level* for every business rule. This enforcement level can make a statement on the enforcement of a business rule. The enforcement level can have two characteristics:

- *Strict*—The business rule must be adhered to. It becomes an organizational procedure (which may be labor law-relevant).
- *Guideline*—The business rule should be adhered to, but deviations may occur in justified exceptions.

Examples for Directives

To continue the previous example, the following would be suitable examples:

- Business directive: "Our ambition is always to exceed the expectations of every customer. Every customer should be positively surprised at least once, ideally with every order."
- Business rule (guideline): "Graphics for publications and training presentations should be created using Visio."
- Business rule (strict): "Employees, who are being prevented from coming to work, must immediately notify the management stating the reasons and the estimated duration."[8]

5.4 **INFLUENCER**

Somehow, everything in this world has some kind of influence on something. Tonight's weather forecast will have an influence on the clothes you are going to wear tomorrow. The book which you are reading right now will have some (hopefully positive) influence on your everyday work. As you can see, we are gradually entering a philosophical level here.

Enterprises Subject to Influences

BMM even considers these topics which are rather part of the humanities. It defines an influencer area which describes to which *influencers* the enterprise is exposed, for instance, current trends in the market, activities by competitors, or the employees' attitude. Influencers can be *external influencers* or *internal influencers* (Figure 5.11).

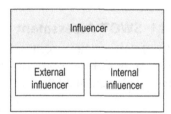

■ **FIGURE 5.11** BMM Area Influencer (Overview)

Influences Justify the End and Means

Naming the *influences* helps you to understand how and why the end and means of the enterprise have come about. According to this, influencers are concrete events that occurred at a specific point in time, for example,

---

[8]Take a look at your work contract, where you can surely find a very similar wording.

the rapid increase in the sales of green power supply products after the nuclear disaster of Fukushima. But influences can also involve facts or even habits (unwritten laws), for instance, "managers are always recruited within the organization." The format of an influence is less important; it is more essential that the influence is relevant for setting the goal, and/or that it has the means to achieve the goal.

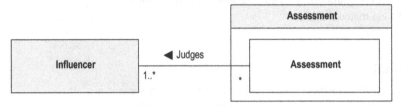

■ **FIGURE 5.12** Influencer (Metamodel)

Initially, influencers are just there—until someone makes an *assessment*[9] on how they influence the end and means (Figure 5.12).

Influencers Are Always Neutral

It is therefore important that the influencer itself is described neutrally and not subject to assessment. As you can see in the previous model, for every influencer there can be any number of assessments which are considered independent of the influencer.

5.4.1 **SWOT Assessment**

The BMM's standard procedure available for such matters is an excellent example for such an assessment: the SWOT analysis, which was already presented in Section 2.1.8.

Evaluate Nuclear Disaster

For this purpose, you select an (external or internal) influencer—let's say "Nuclear Disaster of Fukushima"—and assess its *impact* on the enterprise. For many enterprises, the impact may pose a threat; others conclude that this event doesn't have any impact on their business area, or that provides a great opportunity. The assessment may lead to a new goal for which you must find a suitable means for implementation. The next section provides more information on this.

---

[9]Assessment is a separate area in BMM, which is discussed in more detail in Section 5.5.

5.4.2 **External and Internal Influencers**

An enterprise is exposed to influences from the outside or from within. For this reason, BMM makes a distinction between *external and internal influencers*. Every influencer can be assigned to different categories. The BMM has already defined default categories for external and internal influencers. You can add further categories if you want to (Table 5.1).

Table 5.1 Default Categories for External Influencers

Competitors	Environment
Customers	Regulation, laws
Partners	Technologies
Vendors	

An example for an external influencer (category: competitors) would be: "Two competitors have merged and are therefore larger than the enterprise considered." (Table 5.2)

Table 5.2 Default Categories for Internal Influencers

Assumption	Point of issue
Enterprise value (implicit, explicit)	(Management) privilege
Habit	Resource, supplies
Infrastructure	

A concrete example for an internal influencer (category: privilege) would be: "The management has decided that, in the next three years, expansion in Switzerland has priority over other countries."

5.5 **ASSESSMENTS**

Have you ever been to an assessment center? If not, imagine a row of judges (maybe from sports) who hold up their marks after you've given your presentation. They "assess" you.

Assessments Assess Influencers

This is exactly what happens to an *influencer*, which is a neutral element initially. The influencer is not evaluated until the assessment, more precisely: It judges the impacts of the influencer on the end or the means of the enterprise. The overview of this separate area is rather plain; it only contains one single element (Figure 5.13):

Assessment

■ **FIGURE 5.13** BMM Area Assessment

Assessments as the Connecting Link

This area is not particularly comprehensive; however, the assessment establishes the logical link between the influencers and the end and means of the enterprise. The metamodel illustrates as follows.

An assessment can *judge* multiple influencers (but at least one). This makes sense because otherwise, you wouldn't know what the assessment refers to. In this context, it is insignificant whether the influencer is external or internal (Figure 5.14).

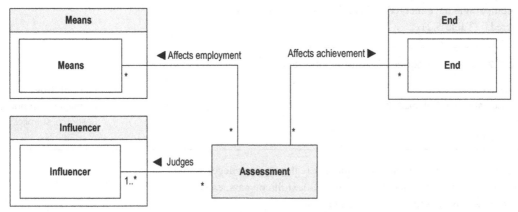

■ **FIGURE 5.14** Assessment (Metamodel)

It is possible that the assessment *affects achievement* of any elements from the *end* area, for instance, goals or objectives, or even the vision. In the above model, the term *end* is used as a superordinate for these elements.

And finally, the assessment can affect the *employment* of any means, in other words, it can lead to new missions, strategies, tactics, policies, or business rules. Here again, *means* is to be understood as a superordinate for these things.

SWOT

SWOT assessment—again? Déjà vu? That's right. So that SWOT really haunts you in your dreams, the following illustrates the topic from another perspective.

SWOT as an Assessment Category

Every assessment can be provided with different categories. If you cannot think of anything new, simply use one of the SWOT letters for *strength*, *weakness*, *opportunity*, or *threat* as the default assessment category—that's what BMM requires.

> External influencer = opportunity or threat
> Internal influencer = strength or weakness

Typically, there's a context between the type of influencer (external or internal) and the SWOT categorization of an assessment. Although this is self-evident, it is helpful to call attention to this fact: Presumably, you would assess the nuclear disaster neither as a strength nor a weakness, but only as an opportunity or threat. Got the context? Exactly. External influencers are rather categorized as opportunity or threat, while internal influencers are assessed as strengths or weaknesses.

5.6 **ORGANIZATION UNIT**

Imagine that you (for whatever reason) modeled an enterprise's vision, the most essential goals and objectives such as missions, strategies, tactics, business policies, business rules, influencers, and even their assessments, and everything just looks great: Well, congratulations!

But what's the use of this model if you don't specify who is to execute the tactics and business processes or comply with the business rules? This directly takes us to the *department* or the *general organization unit* (Figure 5.15).

■ **FIGURE 5.15** BMM Area Organization Unit

The organization units are part of the external information, just like business processes and business rules. Well, at least from the BMM perspective.

Here, OMG clearly delimits the BMM from other standards and, in the BMM, provides for placeholders for other standard concepts.

Logical Links

So it is the task of another standard to describe organization units. But BMM defines how organization units should be linked with the BMM elements. Accordingly, concrete logical links of BMM and organization units are as follows. An organization unit

- *Defines ends,*
- *Establishes means,*
- *Recognizes influencers,*
- *Makes assessments,*
- *Defines strategies,* and
- *Is responsible for business processes.*

Digression Zachman Framework

Within the scope of business process management, the term *Enterprise Architecture Management* (EAM) is frequently used. This involves the enterprise's business processes, as well as the consideration and administration of human resources and infrastructure (buildings, inventory, machinery, and IT) of an enterprise. The originator of EAM is John Zachman, who developed the Zachman Framework for documenting and managing enterprise architectures in 1987. You can find more information at http://www.zachman.com/about-the-zachman-framework. The Zachman Framework provides a holistic view of an enterprise and primarily integrates organizational and information-related aspects. The different perspectives (e.g., what, how, and why) are compared with different levels of detail and roles within the enterprise. The BMM we just considered is used as a business plan, for example, in the "why" perspective, that is, the motivation for a process, and at the level of the conceptual enterprise model. Moreover, the "who" column of the framework considers the various organization units of an enterprise. The "how" column (described by business processes) establishes the connection between end and means.

5.7 LEVELS OF ABSTRACTION IN MODELING

Have you ever been to the Miniatur Wunderland in Hamburg? If not, you may have read about it in various travel guides. There, various scenarios and gigantic landscapes are recreated in model railroad format across multiple floors—and everything is built with an absolutely unbelievable love for detail. This is a great example for a model as a copy of reality.

BMM is also about models—enterprise models. This being the case, it is obvious that the OCEB2 certification program also deals with the rather general topic of abstraction levels in modeling.

5.7.1 **The Art of Abstraction**

In the Miniatur Wunderland, you don't see all the details of reality, which is a good thing. This is because abstractions are necessary to structure complex situations and reduce them to a manageable and comprehensible dimension. Otherwise, you would be overwhelmed by the flood of information.

Comprehensive situations are ideally mapped at different levels of abstraction, where each abstraction level should represent a meaningful view of reality so that it can be communicated easily. Unfortunately, you cannot measure the degree of abstraction, but human beings are able to compare two elements and tell which one is more concrete than the other. This is basically enough to ensure, to a certain extent, that elements of the same degree of abstraction are at the same level of abstraction.

In Figure 5.16, an example of levels of abstraction would be the levels of business processes, business workflows, and business scenarios. A business process consists of multiple business workflows and a scenario is a concrete business workflow.

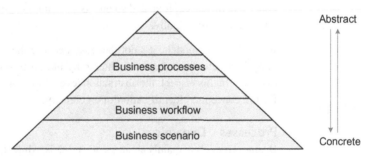

■ **FIGURE 5.16** Abstraction Hierarchies

So if Sam Shark calls *SpeedyCar* to rent a car for the next day, this is a business scenario. The business workflow, however, describes in general[10] how a new car booking is made. A business process additionally describes business workflows, such as changes, cancelations, and billing of car bookings.

---

[10]We almost used the word "abstractly" here.

Getting Concrete at an Abstract Level

The more you abstract (go to higher levels), the more details you must omit. And still the abstraction is to enable added value, that is, it only makes sense if it is still concrete enough. In other words (if you are still looking for quotes): *"Good modeling is the art of getting concrete at an abstract level."* (Tim Weilkiens [39]).

Abstract Models Should Look Nice

At the highest levels of abstraction, the added value mainly consists of the overall view. This involves those nice maps which can be found in many enterprises and are often used to get started. Even if such an "abstract" overviews appear rather trivial: Their development definitely wasn't. And as a structural graphic, a highly abstract model may look *neat and tidy*.

5.7.2 **Static and Dynamic Models**

Whatever topic you select: Start modeling at an abstraction level where modeling seems to be easy. You can use this as the basis for detailing.

Skeleton = Static

The outcome of this decomposition also depends on the type of model. Static models map a specific structure. The human skeleton is a good example here: head, upper limbs, body, and lower limbs. The lower limbs include upper leg, lower leg, foot, and so on. As you can see, you can easily dissect a skeleton—proverbially.

In the dynamic models, it's not that easy because their elements are structured in a network and not in a hierarchy like in business workflows, for example. In this respect, the abstraction levels fulfill an important task, also for the conceptual identification of an element.

Processes = Dynamic

Business modeling mainly creates static models, while the modeling of business processes primarily focuses on dynamic models. Particularly if it involves cross-organizational aspects, then the dynamics are much more interesting than the structural context. Business process models therefore, mainly illustrate activities of people, decisions, and the collaboration of departments.

5.7.3 **Systems Thinking**

OCEB2 REFERENCE

Peter Fingar, *Systems Thinking: The »Core« Core Competency for BPM* [15].

In the upper levels of abstraction, you are quickly confronted with the topic of systems thinking. Systems thinking means to consider the system as a whole. All parts, their connections, and interactions are taken into account. The traditional analysis (Greek *analusis* = a breaking up) breaks up a system into its individual parts and runs an isolated inspection. Systems thinking helps to master complexity.

Google Earth

You surely have used Google Earth to search for your home, right? Starting in space, you first zoom to your continent, then to your country, and so on until you can see your house (and find out, to your own horror that the recording was made last Sunday, because you can see the car of your in-laws).

Everything is a System

What's the reason for this excursion? It wants to illustrate: Everything is a system.[11] When you hear the term system, you quickly think of technical systems. But that is not what is meant here. Everything that you can perceive as a unit of structures and interactive elements constitutes a system. The earth is a system. The United States is a system. And even your family in your house is sort of a system.

In terms of business process management, the systems thinking constitutes the topmost level of abstraction. The enterprise is a system, and the processes are its elements, which in turn, include business workflows and these again are business scenarios.

Organization units, resources, and other things are also integral parts. Systems thinking is supposed to consider *all* elements and their interactions.

5.7.4 **Syntax, Notation, and Semantics**

In order to model systems, you require a modeling language consisting of syntax (vocabulary of the language, including notation and grammar, i.e., including rules on how to use the vocabulary) and semantics (the coordinate and uniform meaning).

The syntax can be subdivided into concrete and abstract syntax:

- The concrete syntax is the (usually graphical) visualization of vocabulary, which is also referred to as notation. For example, you can

---

[11]"Everything is an object" comes from Alan Kay, Dan Ingalls, and Adele Goldberg, developers of the object-oriented programming language SMALLTALK. Today, we're one step ahead.

consider whether you want to illustrate the vision as an eye, and a goal as the bull's eye of a target.

- The abstract syntax, by contrast, involves a set of defined vocabulary (vision, goal, and so on) and its structural context. In BMM, this abstract syntax is illustrated as UML models.

Abstract and concrete syntax ultimately specify how an enterprise model can be described with concrete elements, for example, the defined vision and concrete goals and objectives. The BMM specification therefore contains a model of an enterprise model (hence the root word "meta"). As mentioned initially, BMM does not define any notation (concrete syntax), but leaves it up to you, dear reader, to select the appropriate notations (Figure 5.17).

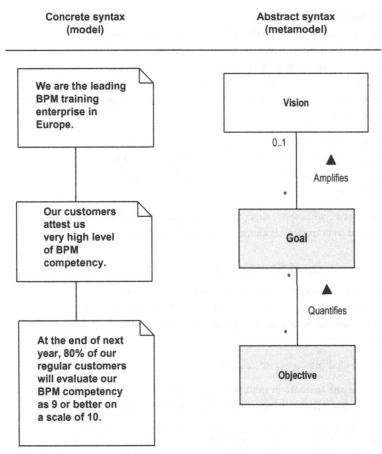

■ **FIGURE 5.17** Abstract and Concrete Syntax

Developing Your Own BMM Notation

So if you want to use BMM in real life, you must design your own graphical notation (sign language). Compared with pure text documentations, graphical models have the following benefits:

- Graphics can be understood and memorized faster.
- A specific perspective of reality can be presented in a targeted manner.
- An existing metamodel already provides a meaning for the concrete model, without having to document it explicitly once again.

Semantics

Semantics describes the meaning and the use of the model element if required.

BMM writes the following about vision: "*A Vision describes the future state of the enterprise, without regard to how it is to be achieved [...].*" This meaning helps us to find the right level of abstraction.

Precisely because a model is always an abstraction, it should always be unique. Well-defined syntax and semantics provide support here. The more uniquely you define the abstract syntax, notation, and semantics, the sooner different users obtain a common, and, above all, holistic understanding of a model's meaning. Therefore, specifications, such as BMM, try to illustrate situations with many graphical UML models and combine them skillfully with natural language.

5.8 **SAMPLE QUESTIONS**

Here you can test your knowledge on the *business modeling* topic. Have fun!

You can find the correct answers in Section 8.4, Table A.4.

1. A car rental company plans to open new branches in other countries. Which BMM element must be used to describe that statement?
   (a) Goal
   (b) Mission
   (c) Strategy
   (d) Vision
2. A car rental company plans to double the number of customers within the next 5 years. Which BMM element must be used to describe that statement?
   (a) Goal
   (b) Vision
   (c) Strategy
   (d) Objective

3. Which aspect best fits the systems thinking discipline?
   (a) Product development and operation
   (b) Abstraction and complexity
   (c) Communication and presentation
   (d) Simulation and optimization
4. What is most important about the semantics of a model element?
   (a) It has only one meaning.
   (b) The meaning is commonly accepted.
   (c) The meaning is concrete.
   (d) The meaning is abstract.
5. Which are elements of a modeling language?
   (a) Abstract syntax, concrete syntax, semantics
   (b) Notation, semantics
   (c) Vocabulary, grammar, relationships
   (d) Syntax, concrete semantics, notation
6. The annual report of a car rental company shows that there is an increasing demand for luxury cars. Which BMM element must be used to describe that statement?
   (a) Tactic
   (b) Assessment
   (c) Influencer
   (d) Opportunity
7. For the first time a car rental company is fair according to slight car damages, like minor scratches. Which BMM element must be used to describe that statement?
   (a) Business Policy
   (b) Strategy
   (c) Tactic
   (d) Mission
8. What are top-level elements of the end area?
   (a) Mission, course of action, directive
   (b) Vision, desired result
   (c) Business rules, business processes, organization unit
   (d) Assessment, influencer
9. How could a competitor be described in BMM?
   (a) Threat
   (b) Actor
   (c) Influencer
   (d) Market

10. Which concept does BMM use to enable large models?
    (a) Separation of concerns
    (b) Decomposition
    (c) Abstraction
    (d) Packaging
11. What is a set of categories for an assessment?
    (a) SWOT
    (b) External, internal
    (c) End, means
    (d) Rule, policy, procedure

Modeling Business Processes Using BPMN

The most pleasant thing is to get what you want.

Bruno Snell

OCEB2 REFERENCE

Business Process Model and Notation (BPMN) [4].

In the OCEB2 Fundamental exam, 40% of all questions refer to the BPMN. These questions are divided into the following areas:

Business Process Modeling concepts (24%)
- What is BPMN?
- Definition and application of all diagram elements of the descriptive and analytical level
- Sequence flows
- Activities
- Grouping elements of a model

Business Process Modeling skills (16%)

This examination typically inquires definitions, symbols, and syntax of the BPMN. Moreover, it uses concrete examples to examine to what extent the reader understands the content of the diagram.

6.1 WHO OR WHAT IS BPMN?

If you take a look at the current notations for business process modeling, you can primarily find three notations: the EPCs (Event-Driven Process Chains), UML (Unified Modeling Language), and BPMN (Business Process Model and Notation).

Do you already create models using BPMN, or do want to use it in the near future? Then the OCEB2 certification is available at exactly the right time.

But before we start detailing the BPMN, let's take a look at the history of BPMN.

OCEB 2 Certification Guide. http://dx.doi.org/10.1016/B978-0-12-805352-2.00006-6

History of BPMN

In 2002, Stephan A. White developed a previous version of the current BPMN in cooperation with the BPMI (*Business Process Management Initiative*). Since 2006, BPMN has been an international standard of OMG. The previous OCEB examination was based on BPMN Version 1.1, which was adopted by OMN in 2008. Since late 2013, Version 2.0 is examined in OCEB2-F. This version was adopted by OMG in 2010. BPMN 2.0 now contains a metamodel (thus the change of name from Business Process Modeling Notation to Model and Notation). Moreover, the conversation and choreography diagram was added to the *process diagram*. There are also further notation elements and additional element properties (e.g., for the execution of process diagrams).

Goals of BPMN

BPMN pursues the following goals:

- A standardized graphical notation exists for modeling business processes.
- The notation can be understood by all stakeholders—from business analyst to process implementer.
- Among other things, the notation allows for the mapping of a graphical notation in an executable XML-based process language—for example, *Web Service Business Process Execution Language* (WSBPEL).
- The notation also allows an interchange of diagrams between tools, using an *interchange format* and *execution semantics* using a *process engine*.

If you sneak a peek at the specification,[1] it provides you with

- all elements of the graphical notation,
- the metamodel as a class diagram, and
- mapping of BPMN on WSBPEL and diagram interchange formats (in the specification's appendix).

BPMN supports three types of diagrams: the process diagram, that is, the operational sequence as a model, and the conversation and choreography diagrams that are used in special cases. For this reason, the focus of the BPMN is not on the following:

Not in the Focus

- Structure of organization units
- Structure of resources
- Data and information models

---

[1]Download at http://www.bpmn.org.

- Business strategies
- Business rules

The next section introduces you to BPMN using an example.

6.2 **IN A NUTSHELL: AN INTRODUCTION TO BPMN**

BPMN claims to be easy to understand. See for yourself if this is true. An example conveys the basic concepts of BPMN, so that you can then directly go into the depths.

Process

A *process diagram* consists of activities, events, and gateways, which a sequence flow puts in a *flow sequence*. Activities, events, and gateways are summarized under the term *flow object*.

Figure 6.1 describes in the BPMN how the car rental company *SpeedyCar* creates a monthly statement for a customer. The monthly statement includes all drives of the selected customer.

Comment

In order to name the individual BPMN elements in the diagram, we used a lot of comments. Comments are indicated with an open square bracket in BPMN and can be linked with other model elements using a broken line—the association.

Start Event

The start event marks the start point of a flow. Events in BPMN can have a concrete characteristic that indicates the circumstances under which an event occurs, the trigger. *Timer*. In this example, the process starts with the start event *end of month*, with the *time* trigger. As soon as the end of the month is reached, the incoming event starts the process, *creating monthly statement for a customer*. A time event is triggered at a concrete point in time—for example, 8/2/2014, 02:14:00 A.M.—or by a recurring time event—for example, at the end of the month. *Message*. Message is another event trigger. For example, an incoming phone call or an incoming e-mail of the message trigger can start a process.

Token

As soon as a start event occurs, the process is instantiated and a token is generated for the outbound sequence flow. A token is some sort of virtual marble that rolls through the process. In contrast to a real marble, the token can

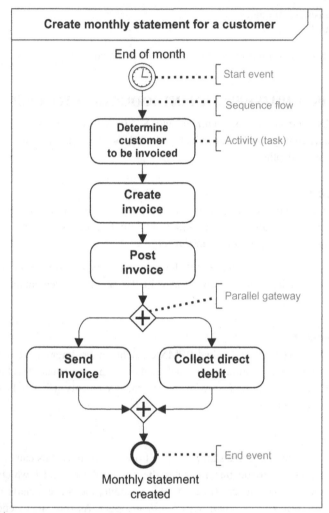

■ FIGURE 6.1 Our first BPMN-model.

proliferate or be destroyed. The instance of the defined process ends when the last token is resolved.

Parallel Gateway

In Figure 6.1, the token runs from the start event to the tasks, *determine customer to be invoiced*, *create invoice*, and *post invoice*, via the sequence flow. After the *post invoice* task, the sequence flow enters a parallel gateway. The gateway splits the sequence flow into two parallel lines, which doubles the token. Each sequence flow receives a token.

The BPMN offers two options to illustrate *parallel flows*: explicit, using a parallel gateway or implicit, using several sequence flows that exit an activity. In both cases, each outbound sequence flow receives a token and triggers the tasks, *send invoice* or collect *direct debit* (Figure 6.2).

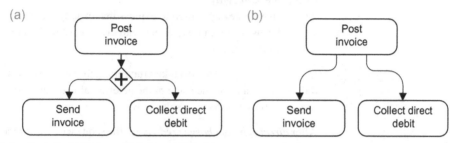

■ **FIGURE 6.2** Branching in Parallel Workflows. (A) Explicit and (B) Implicit

The parallel gateway can split or synchronize parallel workflows. In the synchronization, several sequence flows lead into the gateway and only one leads out (Figure 6.3). The gateway waits until a token is available at every incoming flow. Only then are the tokens joined, and the flow continues.

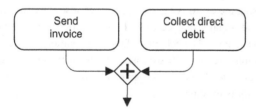

■ **FIGURE 6.3** Joining Parallel Flows

In this example, the parallel activities, *send invoice* and collect *direct debit*, are synchronized in a parallel gateway. Only when the two tasks have been completed, does the flow continue.

End Event

In Figure 6.1, the token then proceeds to an end event, which marks the end of the process and destroys exactly one token. Because no other token is active, the *create monthly statement for a customer* process is completed.

Now, let's enhance the process: In addition to direct debit payment, credit card payment is also possible in future (Figure 6.4).

Exclusive Gateway

An exclusive gateway is used to express that exactly one alternative can be selected. Customers can pay either with credit card or direct debit, but not with both (Figure 6.4).

In an exclusive gateway, the token runs along the sequence flow whose condition is met first. As the name of the gateway already suggests, exactly one sequence flow is selected exclusively.

After *direct debit* or *charge credit card*, the sequence flow is merged with an exclusive gateway again. As soon as one of the two tasks is completed, the token migrates to the gateway and passes it without any delay.

As an alternative for the exclusive gateway, the sequence flow can also be merged in an activity. If several sequence flows end in an activity, each incoming token triggers the activity.

As soon as *direct debit* or *charge credit card* has been executed, the *display invoice type* activity starts (Figure 6.5).

Conditional Sequence Flow

Instead of using the exclusive gateway, you can also illustrate an alternative using the conditional sequence flow. It is identified with a small diamond directly at the activity. The behavior of the two notations is identical, if associated conditions are mutually exclusive. If the customer requests an *e-mail delivery*, as illustrated in the example of Figure 6.6, the *create e-mail with invoice* activity is executed.

If several conditions are true, all associated sequence flows receive a token. The flow is parallelized, depending on the conditions. This is the case if the customer has selected *e-mail delivery* and *postal delivery*.

Default Flow

In case of an exclusive gateway or a conditional sequence flow, you can specify a default flow, additionally. It receives a token if none of the conditions specified is true. You can use the default flow to prevent that the flow gets caught in a branch (*deadlock*; Figure 6.7).

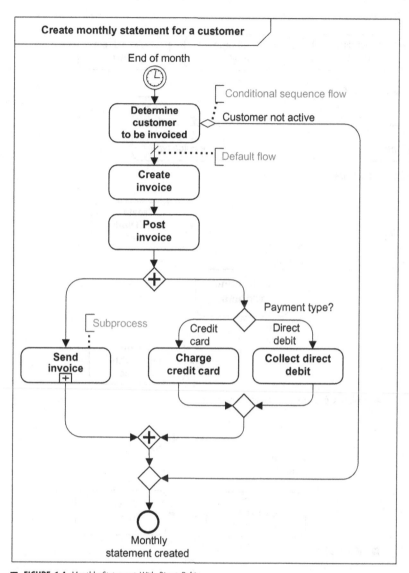

■ **FIGURE 6.4** Monthly Statement With Direct Debit

Hierarchization of Processes

In order to not have to model a complex process across entire walls (in the literal sense), you can subdivide processes. In Figure 6.8, *send invoice* is shown as a subprocess. The "+" sign indicates that the *send invoice* subprocess was modeled in collapsed form. If you expanded the subprocess, the modeling for the subprocess would be visible in BPMN as part of the parent process.

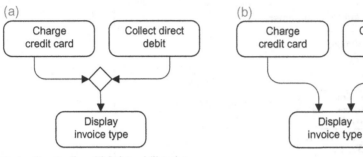

■ **FIGURE 6.5** Merging Alternative Flows. (A) Explicit and (B) Implicit

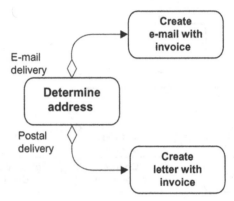

■ **FIGURE 6.6** Conditional Sequence Flow

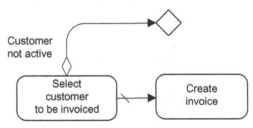

■ **FIGURE 6.7** Default Flow

Data Objects

Processes and business objects are closely intermeshed in business processes. A process works with business objects, that is, it can create, change, or destroy this information, or available objects. In BPMN, business objects are modeled as data objects. Provided that an activity was modeled using an inbound data object, it is not executed until the data object is available.

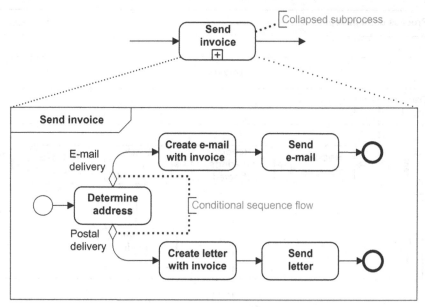

■ **FIGURE 6.8** Subprocess With Detailing

State

In Figure 6.9, the *invoice* data object in the *created* state enters the *send invoice* activity and uses it, which is indicated by the data association connector. The activity then changes the data object by setting the state to *sent*.

Pool

Business processes often involve roles. Pools are used to subdivide a process according to different organizations. Examples include customers, enterprises, or suppliers. Figure 6.10, *process damage report*, includes three

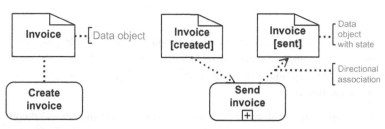

■ **FIGURE 6.9** Examples of Data Objects

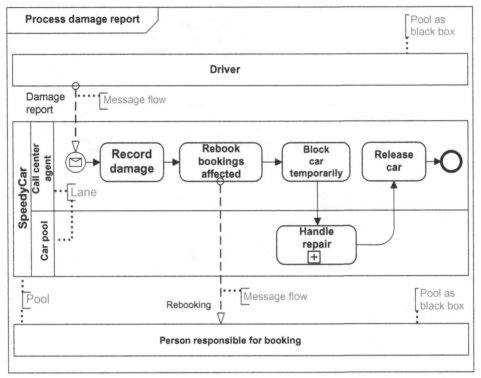

pools: driver, *SpeedyCar*, and the person responsible for booking. ***Black box***. If the flow within a pool is not relevant, the pool can be displayed as a black box—like for the person responsible for booking. The internal flow is hidden in this case.

Message Flows

Every pool is responsible for its process and can communicate with other pools via *message flows*. The driver sends *SpeedyCar* a damage *report message*. The incoming message starts the process in the *SpeedyCar* pool.

Lane

With lanes, you can structure an organization by groups or roles, for example. In this example, *SpeedyCar* includes the *car pool* and *call center agent* lanes. Lanes communicate with other lanes within the same pool using sequence flows.

After this brief introductory example, let's now discuss the advanced concepts of BPMN.

6.3 **TOKEN**

Simulating Flow Scenarios

A process describes several flow scenarios that can be simulated and illustrated using tokens. Moreover, the behavior of BPMN elements can be described well using tokens as little helpers.

Virtual Marble

A token is some sort of virtual marble, which is generated when a process is called and stands for a concrete flow along events, activities, gateways, and sequence flows. A token never crosses the message flow to reach the flow of another pool.

No graphical symbol is defined for the token in the BPMN specification. To illustrate flow scenarios and describe special BPMN elements, we picked a symbol for our virtual marble (Figure 6.11).

The token with number 3.2 is the second token at time 3 (Figure 6.14). The following figures show the concrete flow of the *marbles* process at different points in time in flip-book style.

When a process begins, the start event generates a token as shown in Figure 6.12. The token migrates to the first activity along the sequence flow. Whenever a token touches an activity, it is executed.

After the activity has been processed, the token goes to the next flow object via the sequence flow (Figure 6.13).

■ **FIGURE 6.11** Token

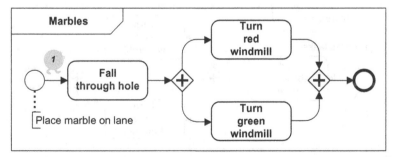

■ **FIGURE 6.12** Place Marble

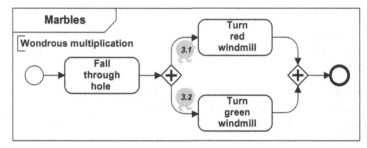

■ **FIGURE 6.13** Process Task

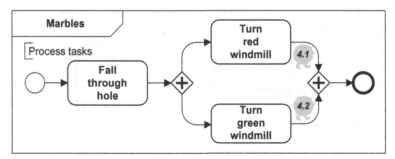

■ **FIGURE 6.14** Wondrous Multiplication

There, it encounters a parallel gateway. Depending on the gateway type, the token exhibits a different behavior. In a parallel gateway, the token is cloned, so that all parallel branches receive a token (Figure 6.14).

Each token now starts its activity. Upon completion, it goes via the sequence flow to the second parallel gateway where the flow is synchronized (Figure 6.15).

Only if a token has arrived at every inbound parallel branch, are the tokens joined into one single token, and the flow is continued (Figure 6.16).

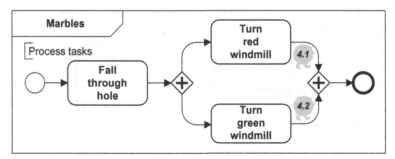

■ **FIGURE 6.15** Process Tasks

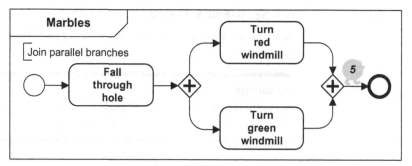

■ **FIGURE 6.16** Join Parallel Branches

The token now enters an end event where it is destroyed (Figure 6.17). If no other token is active at this point in time, the entire flow is completed. So a process is always completed when the last active token reaches the end event.

Figure 6.18 shows the flip-book in one single diagram.

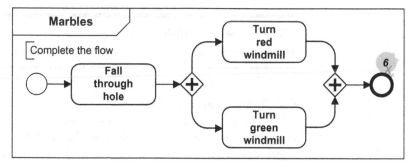

■ **FIGURE 6.17** Complete the Flow

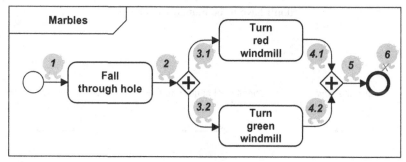

■ **FIGURE 6.18** All Marbles at a Glance

6.4 **SEQUENCE FLOW**

In a concrete flow, a token runs from flow object to flow object along the sequence flow.

DEFINITION

The **sequence flow** links the *flow objects* and therefore describes the flow sequence of activities in the process (Figure 6.19).

The sequence flow is only used for mapping possible flow sequences, and not for describing the message exchange between pools. Sequence flows beyond pool boundaries, between pools, data objects, and comments are not possible.

Two Rules for the Sequence Flow

A start event cannot have an incoming sequence flow. An end event cannot have an outgoing sequence flow.

**DEFINITION**

The **conditional sequence flow** is a sequence flow with a condition.

Conditional Sequence Flow

If the condition is true, the conditional sequence flow receives a token after the activity has been completed. Based on the gateway symbol, the conditional sequence flow includes a little diamond at the source. It must never come directly from a gateway or an event. If an activity has several outbound conditional sequence flows, every sequence flow receives a token whose condition is met. In contrast to the exclusive gateway, the conditions don't have to be mutually exclusive.

Sequence flow	Conditional sequence flow	Default sequence flow
⟶	◇⟶	⤙⟶

■ **FIGURE 6.19** Sequence Flow Notation

➤⟍━━━━▶**DEFINITION**

The **default sequence flow** receives the token whenever no condition of the other outgoing sequence flows is met.

Default Sequence Flow

The default sequence flow is indicated with a slash. If no condition is true at a branch, the default sequence flow ensures that the token and thus, the flow don't get stuck. This can be modeled directly at an exclusive, inclusive, and complex gateway or an activity. Our recommendation: Cover the entire value range at a branch, using the default sequence flow. This way, you avoid flows that get stuck (*deadlock*) (Figure 6.20).

If several sequence flows without condition leave an activity, the flow is split in parallel (see left diagram in Figure 6.21). Each outgoing flow receives a token.

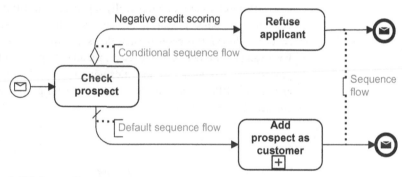

■ **FIGURE 6.20** Example With Sequence Flows

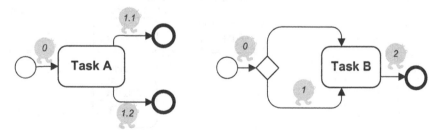

■ **FIGURE 6.21** Parallel and Alternative Sequence Flow

OR Semantics

Watch out! If multiple sequence flows run in an activity, this involves OR semantics! For each incoming token, the activity is executed once (see right diagram in Figure 6.21).

6.5 **ACTIVITIES**

Business processes consist of work steps that require resources and are executed by organization units or IT systems, for example. In BPMN, work steps are modeled using activities.

6.5.1 **Activity: Task, Subprocess, Processes**

DEFINITION

The **activity** describes a work step within a business process.

An activity can either be a task, a subprocess, or a call (Figure 6.22). Processes themselves are not graphically represented in BPMN, but are just a collection of other graphical objects (activities, events, gateways, and sequence flows). Processes present flows at different levels of abstraction. For example, a process can be used to map enterprise-wide or job-related procedures. A sequence of activities within a pool involves a process, for example. A BPMN diagram may include several processes because it can consist of several pools.

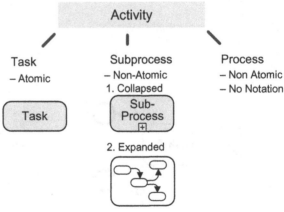

■ **FIGURE 6.22** Activities

Task **DEFINITION**

The **task** is an atomic activity within a process, that is, the task is not detailed as a graphic in the model.

Subprocess

To ensure that you don't have to cover entire walls with complex processes, BPMN provides you with a construct for hierarchization and subdivision: the subprocess.

Subprocess ⊞ **DEFINITION**

The **Subprocess** consists of a refined BPMN diagram (with activities, gateways, events, and sequence flows).

Expanded Subprocess

There are two notation forms for subprocesses: expanded and collapsed. The inside of the *expanded subprocess* includes the detailed flow as another BPMN diagram. A sequence flow must never be connected with the internal elements, but only with the boundary of the subprocess (Figure 6.23).

Collapsed Subprocess

The *collapsed subprocess* indicates a detailed modeling of the work step that was hidden at this point. The collapsed subprocess bears a "+" sign at the lower activity boundary as a marker, which you can see in Figure 6.24.

■ **FIGURE 6.23** Sequence Flows and Expanded Subprocesses

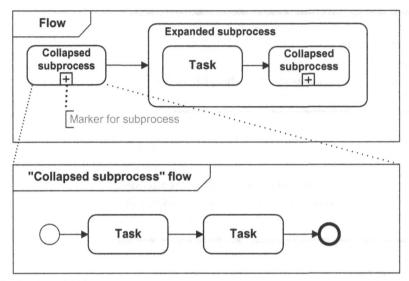

■ **FIGURE 6.24** Collapsed and Expanded Subprocess

No Pools and Lanes, "None" Start Event

The subprocess is embedded in the parent process. Because the parent and child process work in the same global data, the data doesn't have to be transferred from the parent process to the child process. Consequently, the subprocess is dependent on its environmental parent process and can therefore not be reused in other processes. An embedded subprocess doesn't have any pools and lanes. These are defined in the parent process. Moreover, the start event doesn't have any trigger.

Call

The third special form of activities is the *call activity*. It can be used for tasks or subprocesses. A call enables you to call a task or a process that was defined at another location. This element is utilized for reuse. So if a subprocess like *identify customer* occurs in different processes, you can model it once as a subprocess and declare it as "global." You can then reuse it, in other words, call it, in all other processes. All data required is transferred explicitly to the subprocess. As a result, the subprocess is independent and can be reused in other processes. A reusable subprocess can contain several pools.

6.5.2 **Activity Types**

If you want to map an activity with a special behavior, BPMN provides you with predefined activity types. An activity that is repeated several times is an example for this. This activity has the *loop* type and can be indicated with a graphical symbol.

Figure 6.25 provides an overview of all activity types.

"What You Should Know"

You should know the various activity types and their symbols for the examination. For example, you should know the definition of a compensation. How these concepts are used for modeling is not relevant until you reach the advanced examination levels.

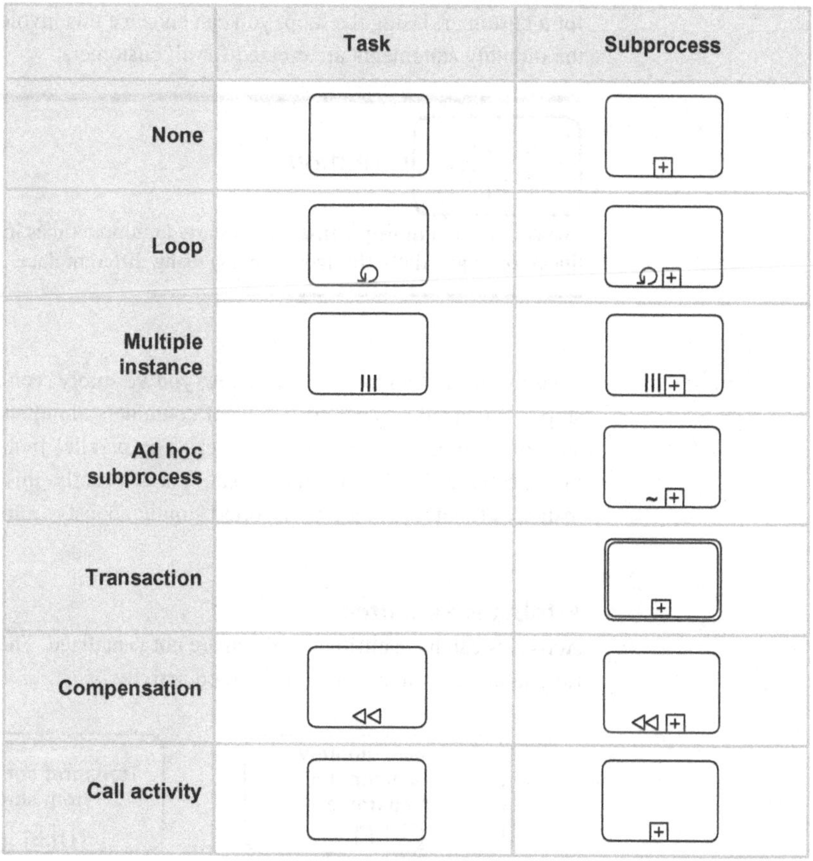

	Task	Subprocess
None		
Loop		
Multiple instance		
Ad hoc subprocess		
Transaction		
Compensation		
Call activity		

■ **FIGURE 6.25** Notation Activity Types

6.5.2.1 Definitions and Descriptions

Loops

There are two types of loops: the loop task and the multiple instance.

 **DEFINITION**

The activity of a **look task** or a **loop subprocess** is repeated until the loop condition is met (changes from true to false), which was defined in the activity's properties.

Figure 6.26 includes an example for both loop types: Figure 6.4 in Section 6.2 already described a flow in which *SpeedyCar* creates an invoice for a customer. Using the loop, you can enhance this invoice flow in which the monthly statements are created for all customers.

 **DEFINITION**

The activity of a **multiple instance** is started multiple times in parallel (vertical lines), or sequentially (horizontal lines) using different data.

If you've ever been to a harbor before, you've surely seen how a container ship is unloaded. Cranes load several containers simultaneously from the ship onto some kind of fork-lift truck. The parallel multiple instance in the second example of Figure 6.26 maps exactly this case. Multiple instances (containers) are transported simultaneously from the ship.

Attributes Permitted

Activities can have attributes, which are not visualized. The *loop condition*, for example, is an attribute of the loop activity.

<table>
<tr><td>Create monthly
statement for
a customer
↻ ⊞</td><td>Transport container
from ship
||| ⊞</td></tr>
</table>

■ **FIGURE 6.26** Loop and Multiple Instance

 **DEFINITION**

In an **ad-hoc subprocess**, its activities are executed randomly—without a predefined sequence.

Ad-hoc Subprocess

You can use the *clean apartment* ad-hoc subprocess from Figure 6.27 to create a cleaning schedule for your partner. But you don't want to give too many restrictions. You therefore leave it up to your partner to define the cleaning sequence to himself or herself. He or she can start in the bathroom, then continue in the living room, and then finally clean the kitchen. Or he or she could first do the living room, then the bathroom, and then the kitchen, and so on. This is how you could model this plan.

Depending on the end condition, activities within an ad-hoc subprocess can be executed multiple times or skipped completely. For example, the executor can decide to wipe the kitchen multiple times or to not clean the living room at all this week. Because an ad-hoc subprocess is a random sequence, it doesn't contain any sequence flow. But if you want to predefine that the kitchen must be cleaned first before bathroom is wiped, you can also use a sequence flow here.

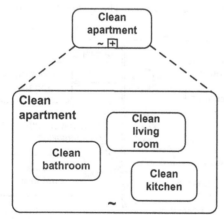

■ **FIGURE 6.27** Ad-Hoc Subprocess

Transaction **DEFINITION**

The **transaction** is a subprocess that must be executed completely successfully or reversed. A transaction is an indivisible whole.

In a transaction, all activities that have been performed successfully will be rolled back if one single activity fails. The failed activity and all activities that have not been started yet are excluded from this rule.

A bank transfer is an everyday example of a transaction. The amount is debited from your account and booked to a receiver account. The transaction combines the debiting and booking into an indivisible whole and succeeds or fails in its entirety respectively. So it can never be the case that the amount is debited from your account without a booking taking place. But what happens if the transaction is terminated? How can you ensure in such a case that a consistent state is reached? At this point, compensation is used (Figure 6.28).

Compensation **DEFINITION**
◁◁

Compensation is an explicit reverse action and describes the steps that are necessary to reverse activities that have been completed successfully.

The compensation's task is, among other things, to establish a consistent state after a terminated transaction. The special feature of a compensation

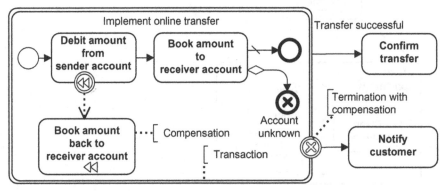

■ **FIGURE 6.28** Transaction With Compensation

is that it automatically remembers whether the associated activity was completed successfully to ensure that only such compensations are run. Compensation can be used independently of a transaction, but it is frequently used in combination with a transaction. If, in our transfer example, a termination occurs due to an unknown receiver account, the token obtains an end state with the *termination* trigger. As a result, the *book amount back to sender account* compensation is called. Consequently, the transaction failed as a whole, and the consistent state was restored. Then the *notify customer* task is performed.

To summarize: the compensation activity describes specifically how the compensation should be carried out, when needed. You can also combine activity types. For example, you can combine the compensation with the loop or multiple instance.

6.5.3 **Behavior Types of Tasks**

Task Types
In addition to the activity type, there are predefined task types that describe the behavior of a task.

Abstract task
With this default value, the behavior of the task is not specified in more detail.

Send task
The send task has only one single job: It sends messages to other external participants (pools). For this reason, the send task must not have any incoming message flows. The send task is an alternative notation form to the throw event with the *message* trigger (Figure 6.29).

Receive task
The receive task waits for messages from external participants (pools) and receives them. Once a message is received, the task is completed and the token leaves the task. A receive task must not have any outgoing message flows. The receive event with the *message* trigger is equivalent to the receive task (Figure 6.30).

Compared with events, the benefit of the "send" behavior type for activities is that the structure in a pool or lane clearly indicates the

■ **FIGURE 6.29** Notation Send Task

■ **FIGURE 6.30** Notation Receive Task

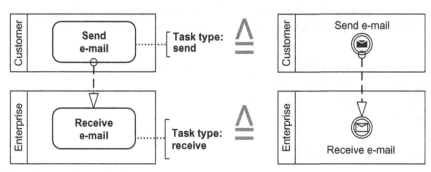

■ **FIGURE 6.31** Behavior Type versus Intermediate Event

executing party. However, the modeling form you choose—task or event—depends on your modeling style and should ideally be specified in modeling principles. Figure 6.31 illustrates the difference between task and event.

Manual task

Filing a letter is an example for a manual task. Manual tasks don't require IT support (Figure 6.32).

User task

A user task is a semiautomated step which the executor performs with the support of a system, for example, entering a PIN number at an ATM (Figure 6.33).

■ **FIGURE 6.32** Notation Manual Task

■ **FIGURE 6.33** Notation User Task

■ **FIGURE 6.34** Notation Service Task

■ **FIGURE 6.35** Notation Script Task

Service task
A service task uses some kind of service, for example, a web service or an automated application. Message flows are permitted to indicate where the service is called (Figure 6.34).

Script task
A script task is run by a *process engine* (Figure 6.35).

6.6 **GATEWAYS**

If a process flow does not only consist of a sequential flow, but if alternative or parallel flows are also of interest, gateways are used.

DEFINITION

The **gateway** controls how the sequence flow spreads and merges within a process.

To map a gateway, you use a diamond symbol. The symbol within the diamond defines the gateway type and thus determines its behavior. A "+" sign describes a parallel gateway, for example (Figure 6.36).

6.6.1 **Exclusive Gateways**

**DEFINITION**

An **exclusive gateway** restricts the sequence flow in such a way that exactly one alternative is selected from a set of alternatives at runtime.

Data-based exclusive gateway	
Event-based exclusive gateway	
Parallel gateway	
Inclusive gateway	
Complex gateway	

■ **FIGURE 6.36** Gateway Notations

Decision

Accordingly, the exclusive gateway corresponds to a typical "either-or" decision where *exactly* one alternative is selected. Or in other words: If multiple sequence flows lead from an exclusive gateway, exactly one outgoing sequence flow receives the token. ***Merge***. If an exclusive gateway *joins* a flow, every incoming token immediately goes through the gateway and continues the flow without delay (Figure 6.37).

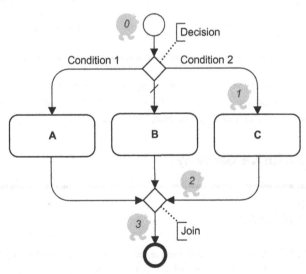

■ **FIGURE 6.37** Data-Based Exclusive Gateway

No Mutually Exclusive Conditions

The conditions in an exclusive gateway don't have to be mutually exclusive. But what happens if two conditions in a gateway are true at the same time? In this case, you as the modeler can specify a sequence in which the conditions are checked. As soon as the first condition is true, the token migrates along the relevant sequence flow. Other true conditions are ignored.

You can imagine that this type of modeling sometimes leads to confusion. We recommend selecting the conditions for a data-based exclusive gateway in such a way that all conditions are mutually exclusive and the entire value range is covered.

There are two types of exclusive gateways: the data-based and the event-based exclusive gateway.

6.6.1.1 Data-Based Exclusive Gateway

**DEFINITION**

The **data-based exclusive gateway** decides, depending on the conditions in the sequence flow, how the token migrates.

The decision whether a condition is true or false can be made at runtime based on the process data provided. Hence, the name data-based exclusive gateway.

Two Equivalent Symbols

BPMN provides two equivalent symbols for mapping the data-based gateway (Figure 6.36). We recommend choosing one notation when you start the modeling.

6.6.1.2 Event-Based Exclusive Gateway

What happens if the process flow can be continued by different events? This case is shown in Figure 6.38. There, a lecture is submitted initially. The process waits until a reply is received by fax, e-mail, or telephone, or the commitment period expires. The event-based exclusive gateway deployed here continues the flow as soon as one of the events occurs.

DEFINITION

Depending on the incoming event, the **event-based exclusive gateway** decides which flow is continued.

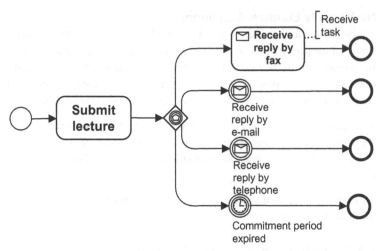

■ **FIGURE 6.38** Event-Based Exclusive Gateway

Response to Various Events

Event-based exclusive gateways are always directly followed by the incoming events or receive tasks. The token remains in the gateway until one of the modeled events arrives. Now the incoming event receives the token and continues the flow. In Figure 6.38, after the *submit lecture* task, the token waits in the exclusive gateway until it receives the reply by fax, e-mail, or telephone, or the commitment period expires.

6.6.2 **Parallel Gateways**

DEFINITION

A **parallel gateway** *splits* the sequence flow into two or more parallel flows or *synchronizes* or *merges* the parallel flows again. The synchronization waits until all incoming sequence flows have arrived. Only then is the flow continued.

Splitting

Synchronization

If the sequence flow is split by a parallel gateway, each outgoing sequence flow receives a token. Conditions in the sequence flows are not permitted. The parallel gateway waits for all tokens for synchronization. In this case, the number of tokens corresponds to the number of incoming sequence flows. It is not specified whether the activities A, B, and C shown in the

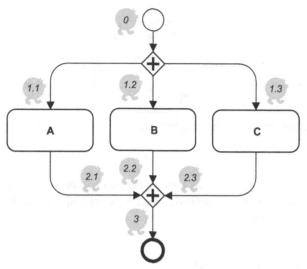

■ **FIGURE 6.39** Parallel Gateway

example of Figure 6.39 are executed at the same time. It is ensured, however, that the flow at the parallel gateway is not continued until all three
activities have been completed and the tokens arrived.

6.6.2.1 Parallel Box

Abbreviated Form

The parallel box contains a subprocess without start and end event. Let's
simulate this flow. The subprocess starts, and every activity without incoming sequence flow receives a token (task B and task C in Figure 6.40). Only
when all tokens in a subprocess have been destroyed, is the subprocess completed. This is the case if all tasks without outgoing sequence flow were executed. As a result, the token leaves the parallel box after task B and task
C have been completed.

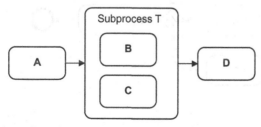

■ **FIGURE 6.40** Workflow Pattern: Parallel Box

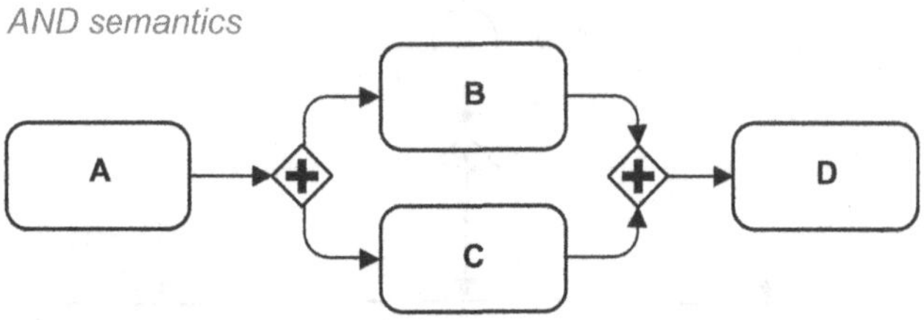

AND semantics

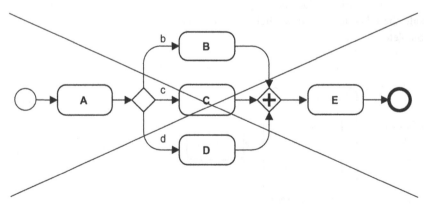

■ **FIGURE 6.41** Workflow Pattern: Parallel Box With Gateways

The same flow can also be illustrated using parallel gateways (Figure 6.41). So the parallel box is an abbreviated form for splitting and synchronizing parallel activities.

"Error-Prone Constructs"

The following example (Figure 6.42) shows—in contrast to the parallel box with gateways—a flow with two different gateway types. It is permitted in principle, that the type of gateway that splits a sequence flow can have another type than the gateway that joins the flow again. However, such constructs are very prone to modeling errors, as this example shows: Because either condition a, b, or c is met, only one token arrives at the parallel gateway. This gateway, however, has three incoming sequence flows and waits for all three tokens. As a result, the flow is never completed. This constitutes a *deadlock*. The gateways that are used for splitting and merging must be checked for their ability to ensure a consistent token flow.

■ **FIGURE 6.42** Deadlock

6.6.3 **Inclusive Gateway**

◇ DEFINITION

In an **inclusive gateway**, the sequence flows receive one or more tokens, depending on the branch conditions.

Decision

If multiple conditions are true at the same time in an inclusive gateway, multiple tokens run from the gateway. If only one condition is true, the inclusive gateway behaves just like an exclusive gateway. In this case, only an outgoing sequence flow receives a token. So the inclusive gateway should not always be considered as an exclusive decision, but rather as an and/or decision.

The following flow variants are possible in the example shown in Figure 6.43. Depending on the condition, after *determine address*, one of the following activities is executed: *create e-mail with invoice* or *create letter with invoice*, or *create e-mail with invoice* and *create letter with invoice*.

An inclusive gateway that joins the sequence flow is a really smart little guy. It knows how many tokens are active and waits until all have been received. Only then does it continue the flow. By contrast, a data-based exclusive gateway would not wait here, but every token would directly pass the gateway and continue the flow. As a result, the subsequent activity could be executed multiple times.

6.6.3.1 Inclusive Decision or Conditional Sequence Flow

To ensure that one or more sequence flows receive tokens in a process, you can use either inclusive gateways or conditional sequence flows for modeling, provided that the appropriate conditions are defined (Figures 6.44 and 6.45).

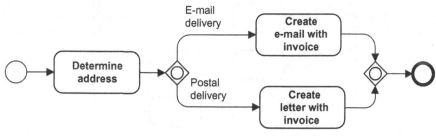

■ **FIGURE 6.43** Inclusive Gateway

■ **FIGURE 6.44** Multiple Selection

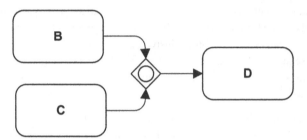

■ **FIGURE 6.45** Joining a Multiple Selection

6.6.4 **Complex Gateway**

◇**DEFINITION**

In a **complex gateway**, the sequence flow runs along one or more borders, depending on the complex branch condition, which is defined in the gateway's properties (Figure 6.46).

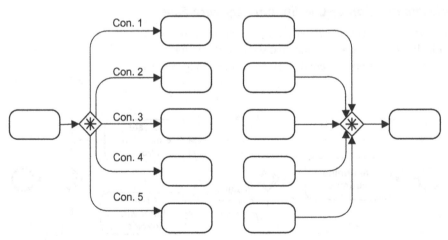

■ **FIGURE 6.46** Complex Gateway

We mentioned the complex gateway for the sake of completeness only; it is irrelevant for the OCEB2 F exam.

6.7 **EVENTS**

Every year on December 31 at 12:00 A.M. a special event occurs that initiates the New Year. Events have a strong influence on flows in enterprises as well. If, for example, damage is reported to a *SpeedyCar*, this triggers the *process damage report* process (Figure 6.10). Events are usually described as conditions (e.g., *damage report received*).

DEFINITION

An **event** is something that happens during a business process and starts, ends, delays, or interrupts the flow.

There are three types of events: start, intermediate, and end event (Figure 6.47).

An event is indicated with a circle, whereas the start event has a narrow edge, the intermediate a double edge, and the end event a bold edge.

◯**DEFINITION**

The occurrence of a **start event** triggers a process and marks the beginning of the flow.

Multiple Start Events

As soon as a process is triggered, the sequence flow originating from the start event receives a token to start the flow. A process diagram may have multiple start events. In this case, only the sequence flow originating from the appropriate start event receives a token. Figure 6.48 provides you with a little example. If a complaint is received via e-mail, this complaint is processed. A complaint received via telephone also starts the process. If the complaint is received twice, once via e-mail, and once via telephone, the

Start event	Intermediate event	End event
◯	◎	◉

■ **FIGURE 6.47** Notation Events

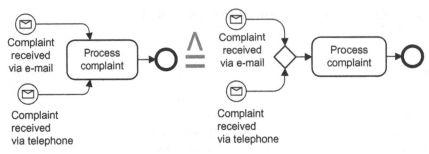

■ **FIGURE 6.48** Start Events

process complaint task is executed twice (in a second process instance, however). By the way: The letter in the start event marks the *message* trigger (Section 6.7.1).

◯DEFINITION

The **intermediate event** occurs between the start and the end event and influences the flow.

◯DEFINITION

The **end event** marks the process end. As soon as all tokens reached the end event, the process instance is terminated.

Multiple End Events

An end event—just like the start event—can occur multiple times in a diagram. As soon as a token reaches the end event, it is destroyed. Only when all tokens have been destroyed, is the entire process instance completed. If an end event has multiple incoming sequence flows, this involves an OR operation. In other words, every incoming token migrates directly to the end event and is consumed there.

Flows With Start and End Event

"All or Nothing!"

Start and end events in a process are optional. But if you model start events, you also need to model end events and vice versa. According to the principle: All or nothing! (Figure 6.49).

How does a process without a start event know which activity is actually started? In this case, all activities that don't have any incoming sequence

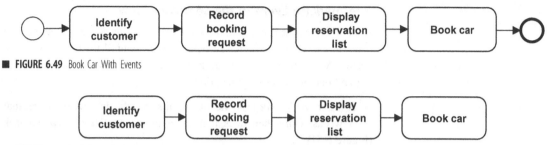

■ **FIGURE 6.49** Book Car With Events

■ **FIGURE 6.50** Book Car Without Events

flow receive a token, in other words, they are implicit start points. In Figure 6.50, the *identify customer* task doesn't have an incoming sequence flow and therefore receives a token when the *book car* process is called. Reversely, each activity without an outgoing sequence flow marks the end of the flow and destroys a token. After the *book car* activity has been executed, it destroys its token. Because no further tokens are active in the process, this ends the entire process.

We generally recommend modeling using start and end events (except for ad-hoc subprocesses and the parallel box) because they clarify the event that triggers or ends the process. Due to lack of space, however, not all of our sample diagrams include them.

Throw and Catch Events

Intermediate events can occur while the process is being implemented. There are two types of intermediate events: *throw event* and *catch event*.

Throw Event

In Figure 6.56, the throw event, *send application*, occurs. When the token reaches the throw event, this event is executed and the flow is immediately continued.

Catch Event

When the token reaches the catch event, *receive application*, it behaves differently. Here, the token waits until the intermediate event occurs. Only then is the flow continued.

The symbol for throw events is complementary to the catch events (Figure 6.55).

An intermediate event can be modeled at two positions: In the sequence flow, or on the boundary of an activity.

Intermediate Event in the Sequence Flow

If the intermediate event is in the sequence flow, the process generates the event at exactly this position or delays the flow until the described event occurs. An intermediate event in the sequence flow has at least one incoming and one outgoing sequence flow.

After the *create invoice* task, the token waits until the time event arrives, that is, 3 weeks. Only then does it migrate to the *receipt of payment* task (Figure 6.51).

Intermediate Event on the Boundary of an Activity

An intermediate event on the boundary of an activity assumes the task of an eavesdropper that cancels the activity as soon as the event occurs. This construct is deployed for troubleshooting, among other things. An intermediate event on the boundary of an activity has no incoming sequence flow, but only outgoing sequence flows. If the intermediate event on the boundary is displayed with a dotted line, it is noninterrupting. In this case, the activity that is modeled after the noninterrupting intermediate event is executed additionally.

An example: If the driver in Figure 6.52 receives the "yellow" sign, he's still waiting at the traffic light, but engages first gear again. Once the "green" signal occurs, he stops the *wait at traffic light* process and continues driving.

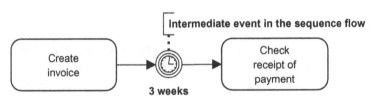

■ **FIGURE 6.51** Intermediate Events in the Sequence Flow

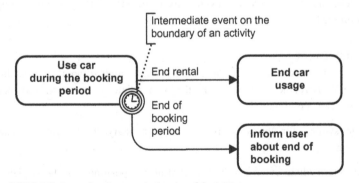

■ **FIGURE 6.52** Intermediate Events on the Boundary of the Activity

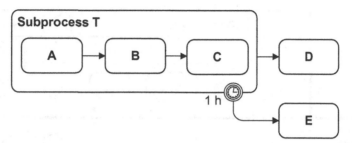

■ **FIGURE 6.53** Intermediate Event on the Boundary of a Subprocess

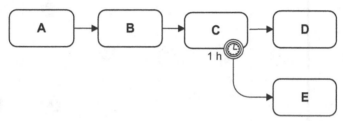

■ **FIGURE 6.54** Intermediate Event on the Boundary of the Activity

"Similar or Identical?"

In Figures 6.53 and 6.54, you can find two examples that seem to be very similar at first glance. But are they really identical? Subprocess T in Figure 6.53 has one hour until it is canceled.

This is different in Figure 6.54: Here, task C may last one hour before it is canceled. In case of a time-related cancelation, task E is executed in both diagrams. D is no longer reached.

Intermediate events on the boundary with a double dotted line are noninterrupting. They trigger another activity that runs in parallel to the current activity; another token is generated as soon as the eavesdropper receives an event. This modeling is often used for escalations.

6.7.1 **Triggers**

The cause for an event—the *trigger*—can be marked with an event type. For the examination, you should know the triggers, *message*, *timer*, and *terminate*, which are discussed in detail in this section.

The symbol within the circle represents the type of the trigger. A letter stands for a message, a clock for a timer event, and a black circle for terminate. Watch out: The timer symbol has its own circle. In this case, the start

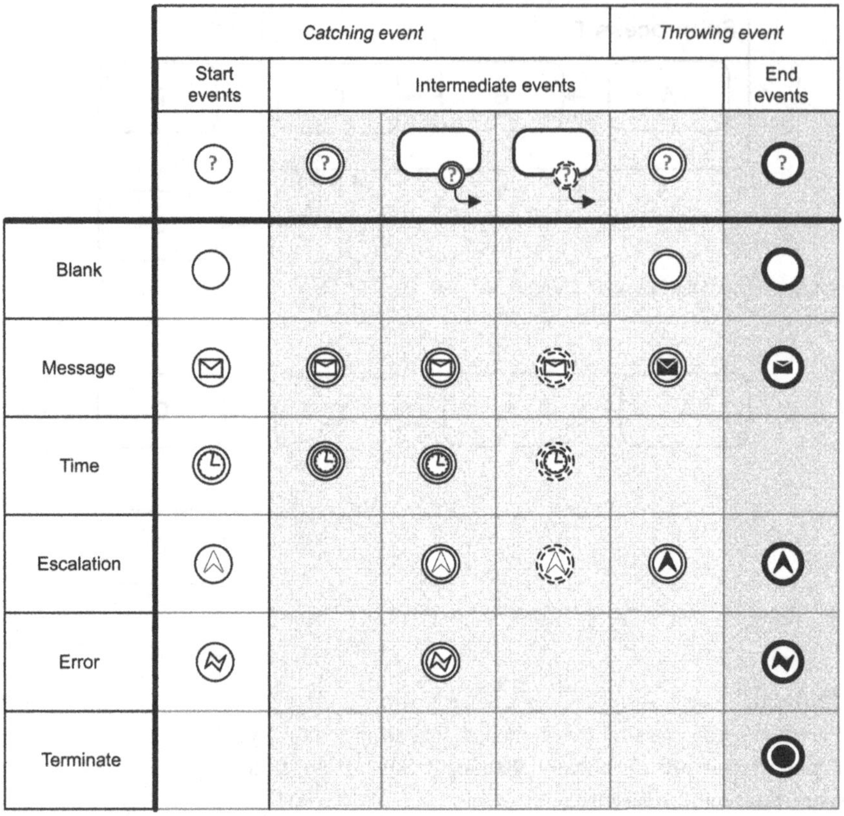

	Catching event					Throwing event
	Start events	Intermediate events				End events
	(?)	(?)	(?) with arrow	(?) dashed with arrow	(?)	(?)
Blank	○				◎	●
Message	✉	✉ catching	✉	✉ dashed	✉ throwing	✉ filled
Time	🕐	🕐	🕐	🕐 dashed		
Escalation	Ⓐ		Ⓐ	Ⓐ dashed	Ⓐ	Ⓐ filled
Error	Ⓝ		Ⓝ			Ⓝ filled
Terminate						◉

■ **FIGURE 6.55** Frequent Events

event therefore consists of two circles and the intermediate event of three circles (Figure 6.55).

6.7.1.1 Timer

An event of the *timer* type starts the flow and continues it when the specified point in time is reached. A timer trigger can be a specific point in time (date, time), a periodically recurring event (for instance, December 31, 12 A.M.), or a relative time designation (for instance, after 2 days).

6.7.1.2 Message

Organizations communicate beyond pool boundaries using messages. In this context, senders and receivers are known. By means of the message, you could even identify the process instance concerned. The *message* event can be used to express explicitly at which point in the flow a response is

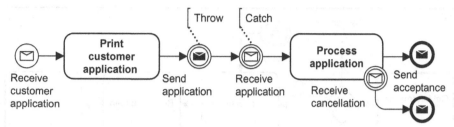

■ **FIGURE 6.56** Add New Customer

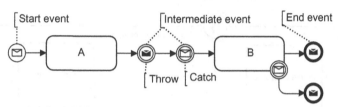

■ **FIGURE 6.57** Events of the Message Type

made to a message. A message can be, for example, a phone call, an e-mail, or a letter. Figure 6.56 shows an example.

Figure 6.57 provides an overview of the permitted usage of message events. For example, if you have an end event with the *message* trigger, the process ends and a message is sent.

Messages can only be used for communication between participants from different pools. They are not permitted for the communication between lanes within a pool. We use data objects and associations in BPMN to express that explicitly and which information or physical objects are transferred between activities of various lanes.

6.7.1.3 Terminate

If a token enters an event of the *terminate* type, all activities are canceled immediately and the entire process ends. This is the main switch of process, so to say. The incoming token and all other active tokens in the process are switched off immediately.

End Event Without Event Type

The end event without event type rather corresponds to a light switch. Only the incoming token is switched off. If other tokens are still active in the process, they remain unaffected and can continue their flow.

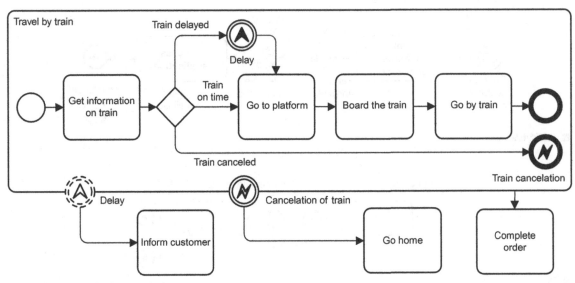

A subprocess cannot terminate its superordinate processes (parent processes) through a terminate event.

6.7.1.4 Error and Escalation Events

As is modeled in the *travel by train* example of Figure 6.58, you can use errors and escalations to bypass possible problem cases. In this case, escalation to the customer takes place if there's a delay and the journey ends, provided that the train is canceled. *Catching* error events are always intermediate results on the boundary of an activity and are interrupting.

If required, you can use an escalation to initiate another process to handle problems that don't result in a cancelation. For this reason, they are usually used as noninterrupting (Figure 6.59).

6.7.1.5 Signal Events

In contrast to message events, signals are not aimed at a specific receiver or a specific process instance and they can be seen, heard, or felt (e.g., light signal, a horn).

6.7.1.6 Condition Events

If a token reaches this event, the event's condition is checked. If the condition is true, the token continues. If not, the token waits until the condition is met, in other words, until the event that meets the condition occurs.

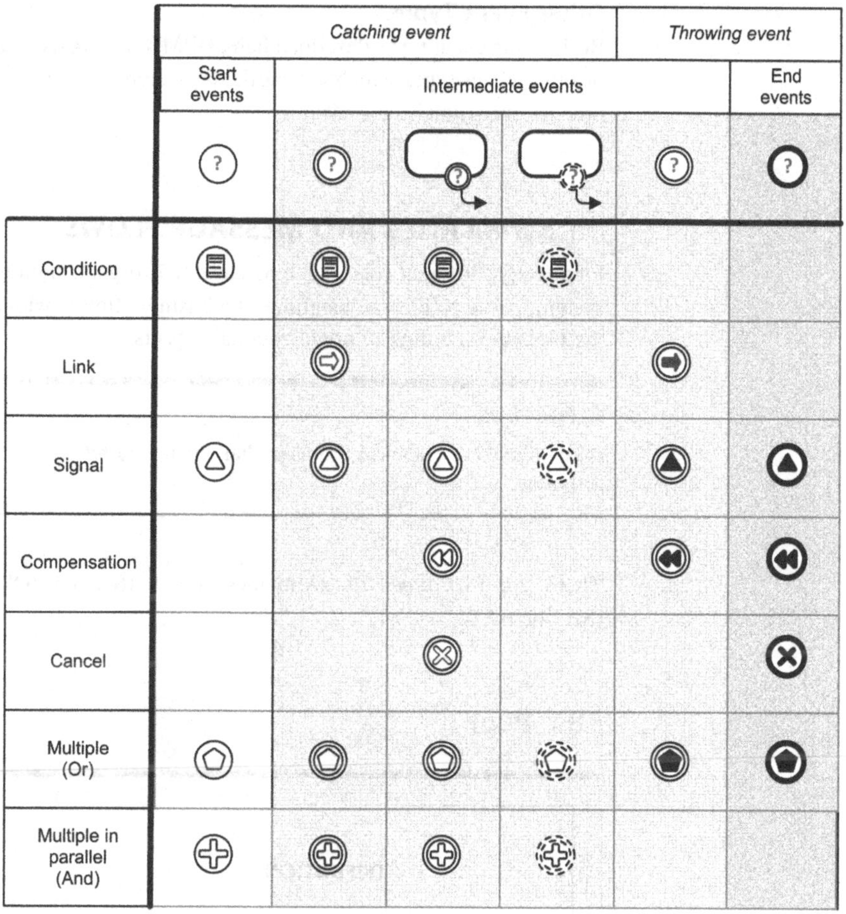

	Catching event				Throwing event	
	Start events	Intermediate events				End events
	(?)	(?)	(?→)	(?↺→)	(?)	(?)
Condition	▤	▣	▣	▦		
Link		⊟→			⬛→	
Signal	△	△	△	△	▲	▲
Compensation		◁◁		◀◀	◀◀	
Cancel		⊗			⊗	
Multiple (Or)	⬠	⬠	⬠	⬠	⬟	⬟
Multiple in parallel (And)	⊕	⊕	⊕	⊕		

■ **FIGURE 6.59** Other Events

6.7.1.7 Link Intermediate Events

Link intermediate events are used to link process parts using a fictive sequence flow. The purpose is to print a process on several pages (*off-page connector*) or map jump labels (*go to*) (to obtain a clearer presentation) if needed. Link events can only link sequence flows within a process and within one hierarchy level. The *source* (*throwing*) is assigned to the *target* (*catching*) using the exact same event name. Link events are always intermediate results, but they are not permitted on the boundary of an activity. Link intermediate events usually occur in pairs. There can also be several sources, but only one target. The source event as one incoming sequence flow only. The target event as one outgoing sequence flow only.

Other Event Types

Besides the event types described here, BPMN distinguishes a whole series of other event types which are particularly significant in the modeling of process execution.

6.8 **SWIMLANES AND MESSAGE FLOWS**

Frequently, different roles, such as customer, organization units, or an IT system, participate in the handling of a business flow. Swimlanes structure the process according to organizational aspects.

DEFINITION

A **swimlane** is a graphical container that separates a set of activities from other activities.

There are two types of swimlanes: pools (Section 6.8.1) and lanes (Section 6.8.2).

6.8.1 **Pool**

 **DEFINITION**

The **pool** represents a *participant* and serves as a container for the sequence flow between activities (Figure 6.60).

Customers, vendors, or your own enterprise are examples of pools. A pool comprises a set of flow objects (activities, gateways, and events) and separates them from other pools.

Pools can be aligned vertically or horizontally (Figure 6.61).

Every process is always located in one pool. The pool representing the enterprise is optional in an enterprise-internal process. As a result, a maximum of one pool can be omitted in each diagram. In a collaborating business process, the participants are modeled using pools (Section 3.5).

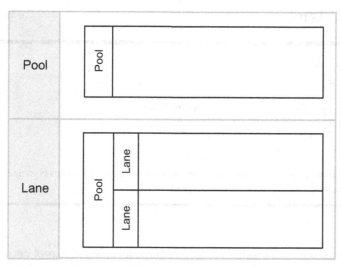

■ **FIGURE 6.60** Notation Pools and Lanes

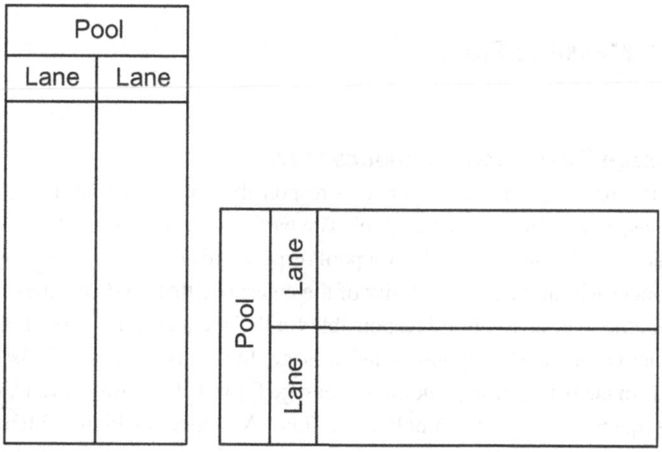

■ **FIGURE 6.61** Horizontal and Vertical Pools

Black Box

If the flow within a pool is not relevant, the pool can be displayed as a *black box*. This way, the concrete flow within the pool is hidden, like in the example of *customer* and *SpeedyCar* shown in Figure 6.63.

6.8.2 **Lane**

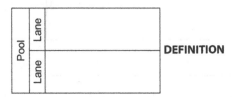

DEFINITION

The **lane** subdivides and structures the activity within a pool. Lanes organize and categorize the activities within the pool.

Internal organization units or roles are lanes, for example. A pool can contain multiple lanes. Lanes can be further subdivided by lanes, too. All activities are always completely within a pool or within a lane. Both pools and lanes can be omitted in modeling. In this case, a process is implicitly within a pool.

6.8.3 **Message Flows**

Message Flow versus Sequence Flow

A participant, such as an enterprise, is responsible for its internal flows, that is, the sequence flow within its pool. The participants use messages to communicate with one another. How a pool responds to an incoming message is no longer within the responsibility of the enterprise that sends the message. Or in other words: Pools are responsible for their sequence flow, but not for another participant's response to its message flow. For this reason, a distinction is made between sequence and message flow. Tokens always run along the sequence flow and symbolize the flow. As shown in Figure 6.62, the sequence flow also links flow objects that are located in different lanes. In contrast to pools, communication between lanes using the message flow is not possible (Figure 6.63).

o— — — —▷**DEFINITION**

The **message flow** symbolizes the information that is exchanged between participants (pools).

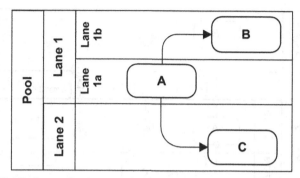

■ **FIGURE 6.62** Sequence Flow Across Lane Boundaries

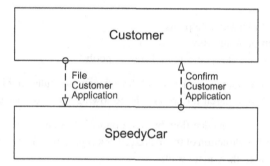

■ **FIGURE 6.63** Message Flows Between Pools

Pools communicate via the message flow only (Figure 6.64). The communication partners must exchange their *public interfaces* to ensure a successful communication.

Connection Rules
The following connection rules for message flows must be taken into account. Message flows are permitted

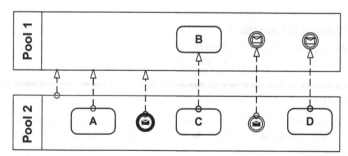

■ **FIGURE 6.64** Example for Permitted Connections

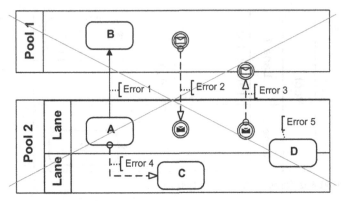

■ **FIGURE 6.65** Erroneous Diagram

- Between two separate pools,
- Between pool and flow object, or
- Between two flow objects in different pools.

Figure 6.64 provides examples for all three connection rules. In Figure 6.65, you can begin to search for errors. The following errors occurred:

- Error 1: The sequence flow between pools is not permitted.
- Error 2: The direction of the message flow is incorrect. It must lead from the throw to the catch event.
- Error 3: Flow objects must never be on the boundary of a pool or a lane.
- Error 4: Message flows between lanes of a pool are not permitted.
- Error 5: Flow objects must never be on the boundary of a pool or a lane.

Figure 6.72 provides an example with pools, lanes, and message flows in the context of *SpeedyCar*.

6.9 ARTIFACTS AND DATA OBJECTS

Additional Information

To enrich a process or its elements with additional information, BPMN provides the concept of artifacts (Figure 6.66).

DEFINITION

An **artifact** is a graphical element that contains additional process or element information, but doesn't influence the flow directly. Artifacts include groups and text annotations.

Group	Text annotation
	⌐ Additional information can be mapped using ⌐ text annotations

■ **FIGURE 6.66** Artifacts

6.9.1 **Group**

Let's take a look at the following application scenario: A sequence of activities that run across multiple pools is to be documented. Because subprocesses may only be within a pool, you require another mechanism here: the group (Figure 6.67).

Groups are used to document related elements.

DEFINITION

The **group** combines multiple elements that belong together logically.

Because a group assumes the role of a text annotation, it has no influence on the flow; it only improves the readability of a diagram. A group is neither a source, nor a target for sequence and message flows.

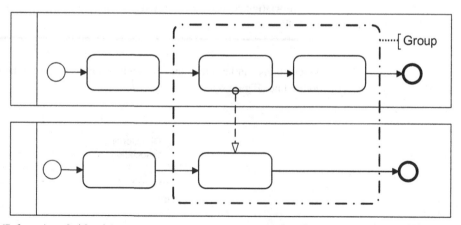

■ **FIGURE 6.67** Groups Across Pool Boundaries

6.9.2 **Comment**

You are probably familiar with the situation in which you properly modeled a rather tricky situation using BMPN and are not absolutely sure whether everyone interpreted it correctly. A text annotation often works wonders.

⌐ Text
| annotation**DEFINITION**
⌐

The **text annotation** is a textual description that can be connected with every diagram element via an association.

In BPMN, the text annotation is represented with an open square bracket and can be appended to any model elements using an association (Figure 6.70). Like all artifacts, the text annotation has no impact on the sequence flow.

6.9.3 **Association**

Information—such as text annotations—can be appended to the model elements to be documented using the association.

--------**DEFINITION**

The **association** connects artifacts (e.g., text annotations) with other model elements.

Associations can be directional or nondirectional, and are modeled with a dotted line (Figure 6.68).

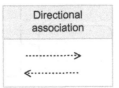

■ **FIGURE 6.68** Notation Association

6.9.4 **Data Objects**

Processes operate on business objects. Data objects are used if it is important which activity creates, changes, or destroys a business object.

Data
object
[state]   **DEFINITION**

A **data object** is a business object that can be generated, required, changed, or destroyed by an activity. Moreover, it can have a specific state. Data objects can represent paper documents, electronic documents, or any other forms of information. They only exist as long as the corresponding process is executed and they are accessible in the process only. Activities must wait for incoming data objects.

The *note symbol* is the symbol for the data object. The state is indicated in square brackets below the name of the data object and is optional (Figures 6.69 and 6.70).

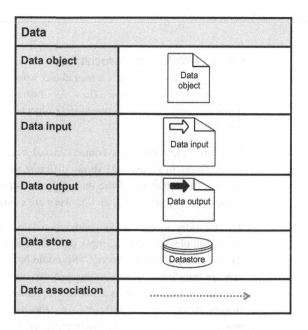

■ **FIGURE 6.69** Data Objects

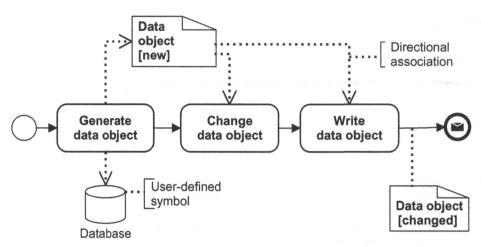

■ **FIGURE 6.70** Data Objects With Associations

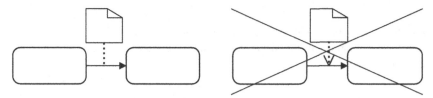

■ **FIGURE 6.71** Associations Have No Direction in Sequence Flows

Connect With Data Associations

A data association connects a data object with a flow object (activity, gateway, or event) or a sequence flow. As illustrated in Figure 6.71, the directional data associations between data objects and sequence flows are not permitted.

There are various options to connect data objects with other model elements. The example in Figure 6.72 shows different variants with the same significance. The notations of the data objects *customer number* and *booking request*, as well as *car list* and *booking* are comparable.

The *datastore*, as well as input and output data objects, are available in addition to simple data objects. Input data objects show that a process requires data as an input for processing. This could be, for example, the parameters that are transferred by the calling process when the process is called as a subprocess. Output objects show that a process produces and outputs data. In contrast to simple data objects, the datastore is also available beyond the process instance. Data can be written (saved) to the datastore, read from the

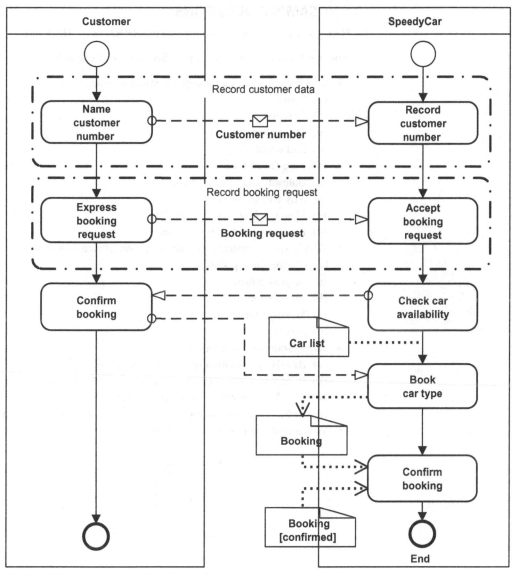

■ **FIGURE 6.72** Book Car

datastore, and used in an activity. The name of the datastore element should indicate the element to be saved, and not the name of the database. The database should be irrelevant for business processes. It is only important which data is supposed to be stored on the database.

6.10 **SAMPLE QUESTIONS**

Here you can test your knowledge on the *BPMN* topic. Have fun!

You can find the correct answers in Section 8.4, Table A.5.

1. Which element cannot accept incoming message flow?
   (a) Pool
   (b) Activity
   (c) Start event
   (d) End event
2. What are flow objects?
   (a) Gateways, activities, events
   (b) Any BPMN element
   (c) Message flow and sequence flow
   (d) Elements inside a pool or lane
3. Which type of connecting objects can connect elements of two different lanes in the same pool?
   (a) Sequence flow
   (b) Association
   (c) Message flow
   (d) Group
4. Which statement is correct?
   (a) BPMN is a notation for business people only.
   (b) BPMN is a shortcut for Business Process Model and Notation.
   (c) BPMN is a notation for IT people only.
   (d) BPMN is a shortcut for Business Process Modeling Notation.
5. Which notation represents a text annotation?

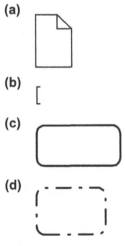

(a)

(b)

(c)

(d)

6. Which is an alternative representation to the given process?

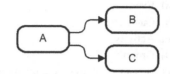

(a)

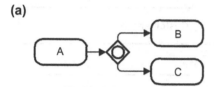

(b)

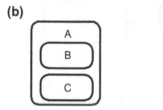

(c)

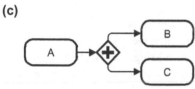

(d)

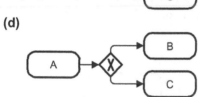

7. Which graphical element describes an association?

    (a) ○‑ ‑ ‑▷
    (b) ⋯⋯⋯>
    (c) ⋯⋯⋯▷
    (d) ⟶

8. Which statement about pools and lanes is true?

    (a) An empty pool is not allowed.
    (b) A collaboration process is a process inside a pool.
    (c) A pool represents a subprocess.
    (d) An embedded subprocess cannot contain pools and lanes.

9. What is a generic term for work that a company performs?
   (a) Event
   (b) Gateway
   (c) Activity
   (d) Group
10. Which statement about the diagram is NOT correct?

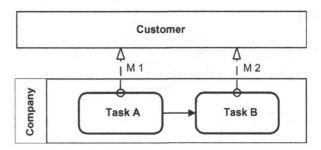

   (a) The diagram shows a collaboration between customer and company.
   (b) The pool "customer" is a black box.
   (c) Message "M1" is sent before message "M2."
   (d) Start and end events are missing. The diagram is not correct.
11. Which diagram describes the interrupt of task "A," if message "M" arrives and starts task "C" next?

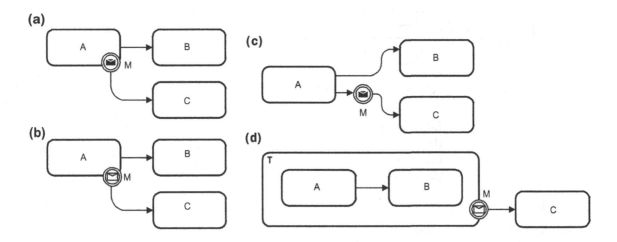

12. At first a customer wants to book a hotel. Then he wants to book a flight and a car, or only a car or only a flight. Which diagram describes this situation?

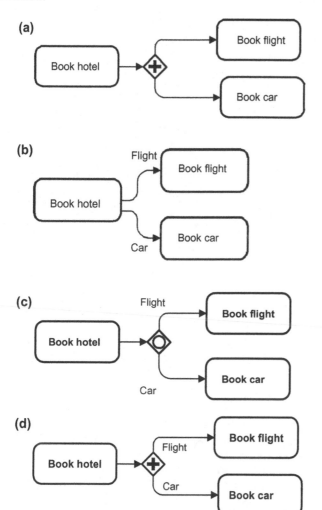

(a)

Book hotel

Book flight

Book car

(b)

Book hotel

Flight

Book flight

Car

Book car

(c)

Book hotel

Flight

Book flight

Car

Book car

(d)

Book hotel

Flight

Book flight

Car

Book car

Chapter

7

Frameworks

Example teaches better than precept.

Samuel Smiles

The last topic area of *OCEB2 Fundamental* comprises frameworks on processes, quality, management, and metrics, as well as regulations. It is not the certification's goal that you know the frameworks in detail, but that you are aware of their existence, and that they can be considered or used in business process management. In your concrete project environment, there may be other frameworks that are of relevance for you.

Overview
Therefore, every framework is discussed only generally. If you want to learn more about these topics beyond the certification, refer to the respectively indicated references.

Terms
In addition to frameworks, this chapter also deals with basic terms from this area, such as quality or regulation, principle, and guideline.

7.1 **DEFINITIONS**

OCEB2 REFERENCE
Dorian et al., Say What You Do [9].

OCEB 2 Certification Guide. http://dx.doi.org/10.1016/B978-0-12-805352-2.00007-8

Regulations, rules, guidelines, and other notations are terms that describe the directives. This section outlines their meaning. The subsequent sections then detail the concrete directives.

Regulation—The regulation is a directive published by legislature and compliance is mandatory. Punishments are possible if they are not complied with. An example for a regulation is the German Banking Law which, among other things, implements Basel III in Germany.

Self-regulatory rule—Self-regulatory rules are *contractual standards* that organizations are committed to on their own accord. For example, credit card companies such as Visa and MasterCard have committed themselves to the *Payment Card Industry Security Standard.*

If these rules are not adhered to, this is not illegal, but it leads to contractually agreed punishments like monetary payments or withdrawal of certifications.

Principle—The principle is a generally acknowledged rule. An example is *OECD*[1] *Guidelines for the Security of Information Systems and Networks* [16]. If you offend against a principle, this doesn't result in punishments, but can have some unpleasant consequences because you depart from a proven procedure.

Guideline—The guideline is a set of principles.

Standard—The standard comprises rules and was created and published by a standardization organization in accordance with a defined process. Nationally or internationally adopted standards are also referred to as norm.

Enterprises can also create standards for their own purposes, for example, to specify an enterprise-wide guideline on business policy compliance.

Control model—The control model is similar to a standard, but it focuses on the implementation of rules. An example includes the *Control Objectives for Information and related Technology* (COBIT) (see also Section 7.4.2).

Best practice—The best practice is the best approach to implement something based on experience. You don't have to pursue this approach and it is not always desirable because it is expensive, for example.

Organizational control—The organizational control is an activity which ensures that a directive, such as an organizational policy or a guideline, is adhered to.

---

[1]*Organisation for Economic Co-operation and Development.*

Organizational policy—The organizational policy is a formal document that describes the organization's attitude toward a specific aspect. It impacts decisions and thus directs the organization into the desired direction. A set of organizational policies of an enterprise is also referred to as a *business policy*.

Compliance with the organizational policy is mandatory within the enterprise. If it is violated, this may lead to disciplinary punishments.

Organizational procedure—The organizational procedure is a step-by-step instruction on how to implement a task. It directly supports the organizational policies and must be handled as such in case of noncompliance.

Safe harbor—Safe harbor is a term to ensure the adherence to regulations. A standard would be an example for a safe harbor. If this standard is adhered to, the regulations addressed are adhered to as well. However, it is not true that the regulation is violated if the standard is not adhered to.

Corporate governance—Corporate governance comprise the set of processes and directives that lead, control, and manage the units of an enterprise (Figure 7.1). It derives from the enterprise's goals and environment, and is significantly influenced by directives.

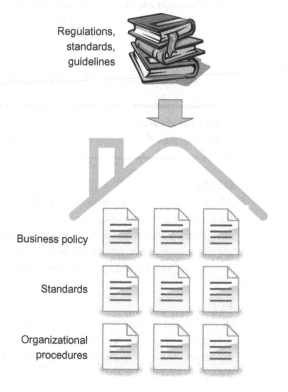

Regulations, standards, guidelines

Business policy

Standards

Organizational procedures

■ **FIGURE 7.1** Corporate Governance

Many of the above terms are used in the context of *compliance*. In business terminology, this describes a process that an enterprise deploys to ensure adherence to laws and internal regulations. The board or management is responsible for compliance. In large enterprises, however, it is frequently implemented by legal departments or specialized staff departments. To support compliance, many enterprises use internal control processes and specifications that are partially derived from standards (COBIT, ITIL, etc.).

7.2 PROCESS FRAMEWORKS

Process frameworks are reference models that support the description, assessment, and optimization of business processes. They usually specify process hierarchies to classify processes. This way, you can classify your own processes in this hierarchy and compare, assess, and improve them based on specified metrics and best practices. It is possible that processes are identified using the knowledge about possible process categories because the process framework reveals typical default processes.

Concrete process frameworks that are addressed in the *OCEB2 Fundamental* certification include *American Productivity & Quality Center (APQC) Process Classification Framework* (PCF), the *Supply Chain Operation Reference* (SCOR) *Model*, and the *Value Reference Model* (VRM).

7.2.1 APQC Process Classification Framework

OCEB2 REFERENCE

APQC Process Classification Framework, Version 6.0.0 [5].

Origin

APQC is a nonprofit organization that offers assessments and best practices for business processes. PCF serves as the basis. It is a category model that categorizes a wide range of processes. Once you've found the category suitable for your process, you obtain the relevant assessments and best practices to compare, assess, and optimize your business process.

PCF

PCF is organized hierarchically. At the top level, you can find two *enterprise level categories*: operating processes and the management and support processes. The underlying level comprises five or seven additional process categories (Figure 7.2).

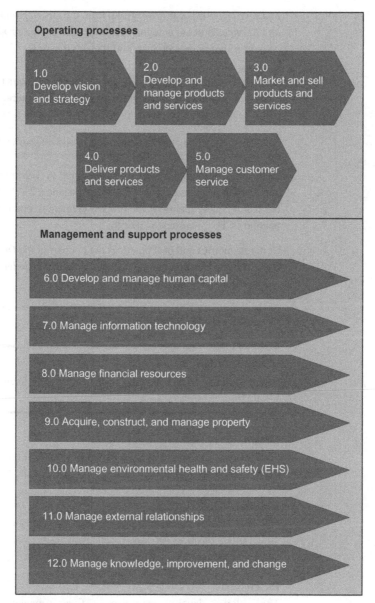

■ **FIGURE 7.2** APQF Process Classification Framework

Each of the process categories includes process groups, and the processes contained therein have a further depth of detail of the activities. In total, PCF describes more than 1,000 processes and activities. But don't worry, you don't need to know all of them for the certification. You only must know what is described here. In the following, we describe the *Manage product and service portfolio* process group from the *Develop and Manage Products and Services* process category including the *Define product/service development requirements* process and its activities:

2.1	**Manage product and service portfolio (10061)**
2.1.2	**Define product/service development requirements (10064)**
2.1.2.1	Identify potential improvements to existing products and services (10068)
2.1.2.2	Identify potential new products and services (10069)

Each process element has two numbers: A hierarchical number that describes the categorization in PCF (for instance, 2.1.2.1) and a serial number that uniquely identifies the process element in other APQC models also beyond PCF (for instance, 10068).

Concrete metrics and best practices are not part of the *OCEB2 Fundamental* certification. Examples are available in the *knowledge base* on APQC's website (http://www.apqc.org).

7.2.2 **SCOR Model**

OCEB2 REFERENCE

Supply Chain Council's Supply-Chain Operations Reference model (SCOR), v10.0 [10].

Origin
Supply Chain Council (SCC) is a nonprofit organization founded by Boston-based consulting firms. It develops and publishes the SCOR.

Standard Descriptions
SCOR is a hierarchical reference model for supply chain processes. The model offers business processes, dependencies between processes, metrics, and best practices.

Processes
The top level comprises five management processes: *Plan ⇒ Source ⇒ Make ⇒ Deliver ⇒ Return.*

SCOR addresses a process chain whereas the five management processes only represent some parts of the chain. The process chain goes from the suppliers' suppliers, to the enterprise considered, to the customers' customers (Figure 7.3).

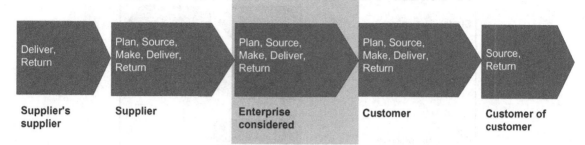

■ **FIGURE 7.3** SCOR Process Chain

Contents
Along the process chain, SCOR considers product movements, the market, and the interaction with customers going from the initial order to payment. SCOR explicitly excludes areas that are not addressed. These include sales, marketing, research, development, as well as some elements of customer service after product delivery. Training, quality, information technology, and administration are addressed in parts only.

7.2.3 **Value Reference Model**

OCEB2 REFERENCE

Introduction to the Value Reference Model (VRM) [20].

Origin
The VRM is developed and published by the nonprofit organization *Value Chain Group*. It addresses the planning, governing, and execution of value chains to promote the effectiveness and optimization of processes. The model supports enterprises in connecting business process beyond functional unit boundaries.

For this purpose, VRM describes reference processes on three process levels each with the three core concepts of input and output, metrics, and best practices (Figure 7.4).

Strategic
The strategic processes are at the top level. They have three categories: *plan, govern, execute*. At this process level you decide how a value chein can be designed to gain a competitive advantage. An example would be a cost-optimized value chain in cooperation with partner enterprises.

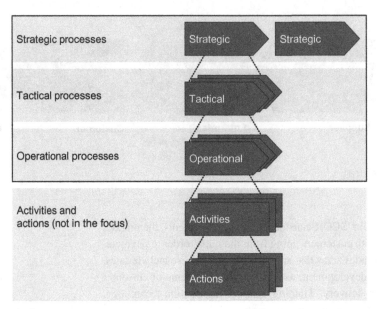

Tactical

The strategic level is followed by the tactical level. Processes at this level implement the strategic plan. This includes, for example, outsourcing of activities.

Operational

The lowest level comprises the operational processes. They are the most detailed processes in the VRM and describe the concrete steps, such as *accept order* or *check order* in the tactical process of *procurement*.

Further levels of detail are addressed, but not discussed further. Activities are refinements of the operational processes, and actions are atomic organizational procedures that cannot be refined further.

7.3 **QUALITY FRAMEWORKS**

Quality frameworks support the improvement or management of a product's or service's quality.

Besides the basic aspects, the following discusses the *Business Process Maturity Model* (BPMM), the Six Sigma quality methodology, the ISO-9000 standards, and the *Toyota Production System* (TPS).

7.3.1 **Basic Principles and Concepts**

What is Quality?

Quality is the central term in this section. But how is it defined? It is frequently associated with the criteria of reliability, usability, and performance. This certainly applies in most cases, but is not directly part of the definition of quality. Quality means to meet the customer's requirements. This can also be obtained with products and services that don't have a high performance, or are unreliable.

Process Improvement

Because the costs for error prevention are usually significantly lower than the costs for error correction, the quality frameworks generally focus on the improvement of processes that directly or indirectly result in the products and services for the customer. For example, already during product development it must be ensured to prevent potential risks and sources of error, and to not *deflect the risks* to subsequent stages of the product life cycle where it would be more difficult to remedy them. Moreover, prevention, that is, sustained error correction, is more cost-effective than regular error controls. Here, too, quality models can support in the short and long term.

It is more effective to intensify the process improvement than to increase the number of inspections which don't detect defects until they have already occurred. Depending on the industry, the focus of process improvement is on different areas. Product developers, for example, should focus on the design processes of their products to prevent product errors from the outset.

Measure and Visualize

To improve processes, you must first identify the weak points. This means that you must specify and measure indicators in order to reveal deficits. For this purpose, you require tools to present the measured indicator values appropriately.

To visualize deviations of measurement points from a specification along a time axis, you can use *run charts*, which are a common quality management tool. Figure 7.5 shows the deviations of the characteristics met from the original booking request at *SpeedyCar*, for instance, pick-up time, car type, car safety seat. They are used, for example, in the Six Sigma quality management methodology (Section 7.3.3). There, they are referred to as *quality control charts*.

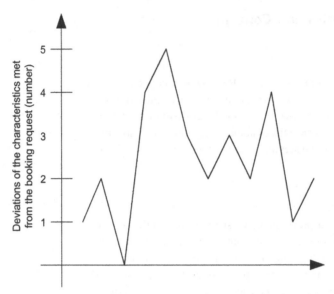

■ **FIGURE 7.5** Example Run Chart

Heat Map

You can graphically illustrate volatile data in *heat maps*. Variable value is identified with different colors. *Heat maps* are particularly known from the meteorology area. There they are used to illustrate temperature distribution in maps. Hence, the name.

7.3.2 **Business Process Maturity Model**

OCEB2 REFERENCE

Business Process Maturity Model (BPMM) [3].

Origin

You are probably familiar with *Capability Maturity Model Integration* (CMMI) [7]. It is a maturity model of processes for system and software development. The successful usage of CMMI at Nedbank Limited (South Africa) brought up the idea of developing exactly the same model for business processes. This is how the BPMM emerged. With some intermediate stops, the maturity model was passed over to OMG that now assumes responsibility.

Watts Humphrey

Watts Humphrey laid the groundwork for maturity models. In the late 1980s, he developed the *process maturity framework* at Software Engineering Institute (SEI). This formed the basis for the *Capability Maturity Model* (CMM) for software in the mid-1990s and the successor CMMI in early 2000. Due to the common history, BPMM is similar to CMMI.

Maturity Levels

A total of five maturity levels exist in BPMM (Table 7.1). Maturity levels 2 through 5 define process groups. These process groups must meet the goals of the corresponding maturity level, in order to reach it. These are best practices that describe what needs to be done. However, they don't outline how this is achieved in practice. BPMM doesn't provide any methods.

Table 7.1 BPMM Maturity Level

Maturity Level	Description
1—*Initial*	The lowest level only implies that business processes exist. They are performed ad hoc, and their results are barely predictable
2—*Managed*	Business processes can be repeated at the local level, that is, specific departments or teams (*work units*) are able to implement defined flows repeatedly. Similar tasks in different teams can be processed with completely different approaches
3—*Standardized*	Standard processes that were derived from best practices, as well as directives exist of how to adapt processes to specific needs
4—*Predictable*	The performance of standard processes is recorded statistically to detect deviations. The further course of the process can be predicted based on the intermediate states
5—*Innovative*	Innovative improvement measures are actively taken to enable the enterprise to achieve its goals

Process Group

A maturity level is not a universal solution that addresses all business processes of an enterprise. Maturity level 2, for example, includes requirements and configuration management, and 7 further processes areas.

Compliance

Appraisal teams determine whether concrete business processes of an enterprise comply with a maturity level of BPMM. These teams consist of an external team leader and team members, some of them working for the enterprise appraised. The appraisers review process artifacts and interview process managers as well as persons that execute the process. There are four different types of *appraisals*:

1. *Starter appraisal*—The appraisal only takes a few days to obtain an overview as to what extent the business processes of an enterprise comply with BPMM. Quantitative data is determined.
2. *Progress appraisal*—All process areas of a maturity level are examined in detail to advance development towards a maturity level or anticipate results of a *confirmatory appraisal*. Quantitative data is determined and compared with the review's results.
3. *Supplier appraisal*—This appraisal is identical to the *progress appraisal*, except that no employees of the enterprise examined are members of the appraisal team.
4. *Confirmatory appraisal*—All stipulated practices of a maturity level are checked in detail and examined with regard to the requested process goals of the maturity level. An organization can advertise the maturity level if it passes this appraisal successfully.

7.3.3 **Six Sigma**

OCEB2 REFERENCE

C. Gygi et al., Six Sigma for Dummies [13].

Six Sigma is a comprehensive methodology for quality improvement. Only a few selected characteristics are part of the *Fundamental* level of OCEB2. Further elements are addressed in the *Intermediate* and *Advanced* levels of OCEB2.

Origin

Six Sigma was developed by Motorola in the mid-1980s. In 1996, Six Sigma attracted great attention when Jack Welch successfully implemented it at General Electric.

Process Improvement

The focus of Six Sigma is on the improvement of processes that result in products and services. For this purpose, Six Sigma provides comprehensive measures whose introduction and implementation require an appropriate infrastructure within the enterprise. The enterprise goals and strategies must be revised, and they require new and adapted role descriptions.

Belts

The role names of Six Sigma are based on ranks used in Japanese martial arts. Figure 7.6 shows the hierarchy of Six Sigma roles. The *Program Manager* is responsible for the introduction and implementation of Six Sigma. Six Sigma Champions promote the Six Sigma program. They establish the new way of thinking and are responsible, for example, for assigning the Black Belt, Green Belt, and Yellow Belt roles. The Master Black Belt is an experienced Six Sigma expert who works as a coach and trainer of the Six Sigma project. The Black Belt roles are experienced Six Sigma users who usually manage Six Sigma projects. Green Belts are leaders in Six Sigma projects. Yellow Belts support Black and Green Belts. They can also implement small projects independently. The hierarchy of roles reflects the requested Six Sigma capabilities.

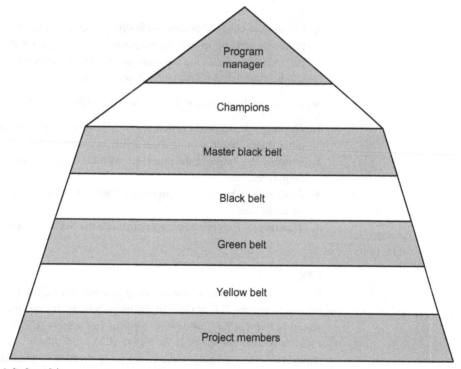

■ **FIGURE 7.6** Six Sigma Roles

DMAIC

The core process of Six Sigma for process improvement comprises five steps. This process is named DMAIC after the initial letters of the process steps.

1. Define the improvement goals—Before you can implement concrete improvement measures, you must first define the goals for improvement. You should only set off if you know where you want to go. Only then can you determine at the end whether you really reached your goal.
2. Measure the current process—In the second step, you collect data on the actual processes. You measure various characteristics to be able to assess the current performance of the processes.
3. Analyze the process—You know your improvement goal and the status quo of the actual processes. On this basis, you can analyze the process and reveal improvement potential.
4. Improve the process—An effective improvement must be prepared well. Therefore, the actual process improvement is in the fourth position of the Six Sigma process. In this step, you implement the improvement measures.
5. Control the changed process—Finally, you control the changed processes actively so that the measures have a long-term effect. This particularly includes the standardization of new measures so that they can be established permanently in the enterprise.

Six Sigma can be applied in four areas with different focus areas.

1. *Thinking*—Increase the efficiency of individual employees, among other things, by promoting their ability to assess things.
2. *Processing*—Improve the processes with the involvement of all employees.
3. *Designing*—Develop new processes. Only a few employees must be involved here.
4. *Managing*—Executive managers manage the Six Sigma program.

CTX

In Six Sigma, a quality characteristic is referred to as CTX. CT stands for *critical to* and the X is in place of the characteristic. In concrete terms, this would be *Critical To Cost* (CTC),[2] *Critical To Delivery* (CTD), *Critical To Process* (CTP), and *Critical To Safety* (CTS). *SpeedyCar*, for example, deploys CTD of how long it takes from the application of admission to confirmation for a new customer account. The enterprise specifies a target for the CTD. Typically, this target is not always adhered to exactly in real life. The tolerance area is specified with upper and lower limits with reference to the CTD.

---

[2]CTC sometimes also stands for *Critical to Customer*.

Process Management Summary

The CTX is presented collectively in the *process management summary*. This is a tool of process monitoring to make all critical process output parameters that decide on the quality visible, and therefore manageable.

Quality Control Chart

The *quality control charts* show an individual quality characteristic along a time-dependent course. They are a variant of the *run charts* (see Section 7.3).

UCL, LCL

The *Upper Control Limit* (UCL) and the *Lower Control Limit* (LCL) form a corridor within which the quality characteristic meets the desired value or a *common cause of variation* (Figure 7.7). Outside the limitations of UCL and LCL, the quality measured is considered as abnormal and requires an intervention in the relevant process.

The unusual name Six Sigma relates to the deviation from the target value of a quality characteristic. Sigma (Greek letter σ) refers to the standard deviation from the mean value. Six Sigma therefore stands for six standard deviations. This is the required minimum clearance of the tolerance limit. If this condition is met, this means that a degree of perfection of almost 100% is in place.

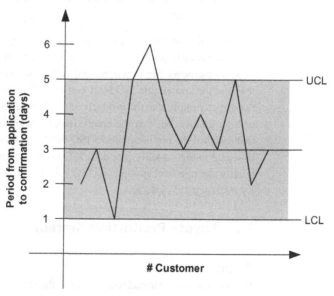

■ **FIGURE 7.7** Example of Quality Control Chart

DPMO

The measurement unit for quality is DPMO (*Defects per Million Opportu-nities*). A process with 3.4 DPMO identifies the Six Sigma process quality. This means that only 3.4 defective results exist in 1 million opportunities.

Process Control Plan

The quality characteristics are output parameters of processes and directly depend on the input parameters. From the mathematical perspective, the following formula applies: $y = f(x) + \epsilon$, where y is the process output parameter (CTX), x the process input parameter, $f()$ the process, and ϵ the uncertainty or deviation. The process management summary monitors the process output parameters, and the *process control plan* maps the process input parameters.

7.3.4 **ISO 9000 et al.**

OCEB2 REFERENCE

Dorian J Cougias et al., Say What You Do: Building a Framework of IT Controls, Policies, Standards, and Procedures [9].

ISO 9000 standards specify a set of *guidelines* for quality improvement. The ISO 9000 series includes the standards ISO 9000, ISO 9001, ISO 9004, as well as ISO 19011.

ISO 9000 defines basic principles and terms of quality improvement. ISO 9001 specifies requirements on a quality management system. If an enterprise implements the requirements, which are confirmed in an audit, it may use the known title ISO 9001 certified. However, the certification does not directly imply that the products or services of the certified enterprise are of high quality, but that the enterprise uses a quality management system that satisfies the requirements of ISO 9001. This should—but doesn't have to—lead to high-quality products. ISO 9004 is a guideline for improving a quality management system, and ISO 19011 is a guideline for auditing quality management systems.

7.3.5 **Toyota Production System**

Origin

Because the Japanese had to accomplish the reconstruction on their own initiative after World War II, many effective procedures originate from this country, or fell on fertile ground there.

The TPS is a procedure for series production developed by Toyota. The goal of TPS is the productivity of mass production in combination with the quality of shop production. TPS is better known as *Just-in-Time* (JIT) production, which addresses a central strategy of TPS.

TPS avoids the storage of resources in the product development process. This is implemented, for example, with the *zero stock* concept, where no resources are kept in stock at all, but are purchased as needed.

7.4 REGULATIONS AND GOVERNANCE FRAMEWORKS

OCEB2 REFERENCE

Dorian J Cougias et al., Say What You Do: Building a Framework of IT Controls, Policies, Standards, and Procedures [9].

Regulation

Regulations are statutory provisions. The business processes must adhere to them or new business processes must be implemented, due to regulations. The regulations addressed by *OCEB2 Fundamental* refer to the financial industry only. Here, it is representative for further regulations from other industries. If you deal with your business processes, you must inform yourself about the relevant provisions and take them into account.

Governance Framework

Governance frameworks specify how processes can be governed. Here, we only consider the governance framework, COBIT.

7.4.1 Sarbanes-Oxley Act

History

Sarbanes-Oxley Act (SOX) was issued after the accounting scandals of the US companies, Enron and WorldCom. The goal of this federal act is to ensure the correctness and reliability of published financial data of enterprises whose stocks are dealt on the US stock exchanges. It primarily makes sure to incorporate the responsibility for correct publishing of financial data at the executive level. In support of this, SOX refers to the audit standard of the "Public Company Accounting Oversight Board."

SOX is named after its sponsors Paul S. Sarbanes and Michael Oxley (committee chairmen).

7.4.2 **Control Objectives for Information and Related Technology**

History

COBIT was developed by the Information Systems Audit and Control Association (ISACA) and the IT Governance Institute, and was published for the first time in 1996. It comprises a range of best practices for IT management and controlling. COBIT links enterprise-wide governance frameworks with IT-specific models, such as ITIL.

COBIT is a top-down approach from the enterprise goals, to the derived IT goals, to the impacts on IT architecture. The achievement of goals is measured respectively, and thus results in a control loop.

COBIT defines a total of 34 IT processes and allocates them via 200 *control objectives*. Process and control objectives, activities, measurement parameters, and guidelines are described for each IT process.

ISACA also published instructions on how COBIT can be used particularly in the environment of SOX implementations.[3]

7.5 **MANAGEMENT FRAMEWORKS**

Management frameworks specify best practices, guidelines, and tools that support the management in its management and monitoring tasks.

7.5.1 **Balanced Scorecards**

OCEB2 REFERENCE

Robert S. Kaplan, David P. Norton, *The Balanced Scorecard* [25].

Balanced Scorecards (BSC) are a management framework that was developed by Robert S. Kaplan and David P. Norton in 1992. It is used to compare the measured key figures with the visions and strategies of the enterprise. *Balanced* refers to the balance between external and internal key figures. The management takes into account the customers and shareholders, but also the internal processes and the further development of the enterprise.

---

[3]http://www.isaca.org/cobit.

The key figures of BSC are referred to as *Key Performance Indicators* (KPI). They are described in more detail in Section 7.5.2. In summary, this forms a key figure system—the *scorecard*—that is subdivided into four perspectives:

- Financial perspective—The shareholders' view focuses on the financial success.
- Customer perspective—The customers' perspective focuses on the vision of the enterprise.
- Internal business process perspective—The internal business process perspective focuses on the business processes that are necessary to meet the shareholders' and customers' expectations.
- Learning and growth perspective—The learning and growth perspective focuses on the enterprise's ability to change and improve in order to reach the vision.

BSC is considered as a strategic management system which supports the critical management processes (Figure 7.8).

7.5.2 **Key Performance Indicator**

OCEB2 REFERENCE

Ed Walters, *What are CSFs and KPIs?* [38].

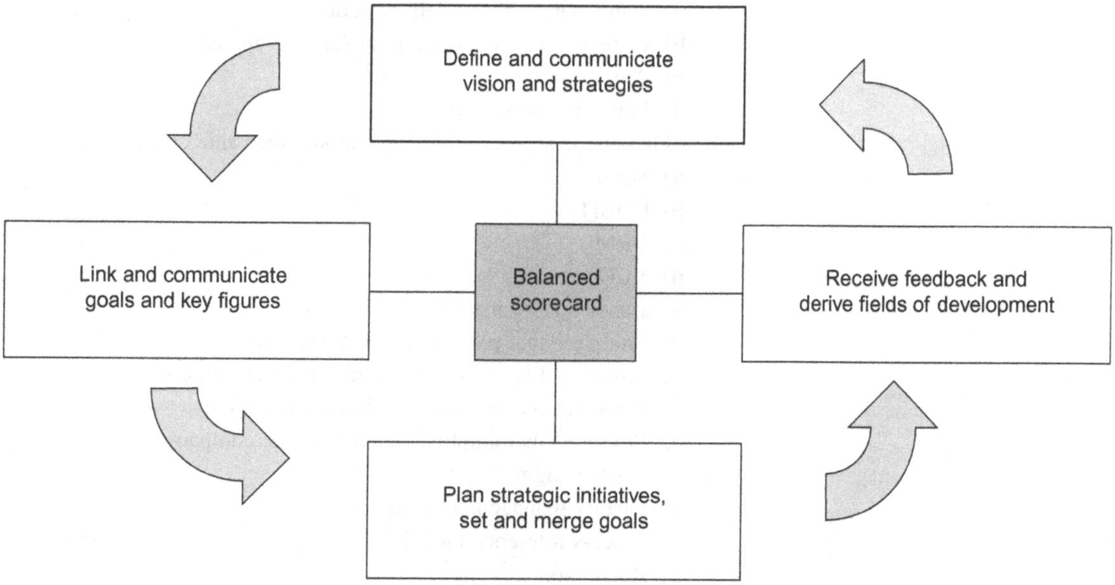

■ **FIGURE 7.8** BSC as a Strategic Management System

KPI and CSF

The KPI is a business metric that measures the degree of fulfillment of a goal or a *Critical Success Factor* (CSF). The CSF is an organization-internal or organization-external property that is necessary to achieve a specific goal. A CSF can involve multiple KPIs.

Example

Let's assume that your goal is to increase your average yield per customer from $10 to $15 by the end of the year. A CSF can be the marketing of a new product, which hopefully has the result that customers spend more money on the enterprise. In this example, the KPI can directly address the degree of fulfillment of the goal. This would be the average yield per customer.

7.6 **SAMPLE QUESTIONS**

Here you can test your knowledge on the *frameworks* topic. Have fun!

You can find the correct answers in Section A.4, Table A.6.

1. Which BPMM level certifies predictable business processes?
    (a) Level 5
    (b) Level 2
    (c) Level 4
    (d) Level 3
2. What are the top level processes of SCOR?
    (a) Plan, source, make, deliver, return
    (b) Concept, analysis, design, implement, operate
    (c) Plan, produce, deliver, return
    (d) Manage, operate, supply
3. Which one is a process reference model for value chain processes?
    (a) SCOR
    (b) COBIT
    (c) VRM
    (d) VCG
4. What does quality mean?
    (a) Processes that perform without any errors
    (b) Processes that satisfy the needs of the customers
    (c) Processes that are optimized and predictable
    (d) Processes that amplify the goals of the company
5. What is Six Sigma?
    (a) Quality management method
    (b) Process reference model
    (c) Regulation
    (d) Management framework

6. The Just-in-Time production belongs to which method?
   (a) Six Sigma
   (b) TPS
   (c) COBIT
   (d) ISO 9000 ff

7. What is addressed by ISO 9004?
   (a) Quality concepts
   (b) Requirements for a quality management system
   (c) Guidelines to improve a quality management system
   (d) Quality maturity model for processes

8. Which domain is addressed by the Sarbanes-Oxley act?
   (a) Healthcare
   (b) Automotive
   (c) Government
   (d) Finance

9. Which one is a collection of best practices for IT management and controlling?
   (a) SCOR
   (b) Six Sigma
   (c) COBIT
   (d) TPS

10. The process category *Manage information technology* is part of which process type in the APQC PCF?
   (a) Operating processes
   (b) Business processes
   (c) Management and support processes
   (d) Infrastructure processes

11. What was developed by Robert S. Kaplan and David P. Norton?
   (a) Business Process Maturity Model
   (b) Balanced Scorecards
   (c) Business Process Reengineering
   (d) Six Sigma

12. What describes a feature that is necessary to achieve a goal?
   (a) Key Performance Indicator
   (b) Business Process Metric
   (c) Maturity Level
   (d) Critical Success Factor

The important thing is to never stop asking questions.

Albert Einstein

A.1 **COVERAGE MAP OCEB2 FUNDAMENTAL**

This section includes the official coverage map of the OCEB2 Fundamental certification [36]. There are seven topic fields in total. Each percentage indicates the weighting in the certification process.

1. **Business goals, objectives** (8%) $\Rightarrow$ Chapter 2:
   - Business basics
   - Strategies, planning, and goal-setting
   - Project management, marketing, personnel management, and finance
2. **Business process concepts and fundamentals** (11%) $\Rightarrow$ Chapter 3:
   Fundamental aspects of business processes:
   - Characteristics of processes
   - Discovering business processes
   - As-is process vs. to-be process
   - Levels of business process modeling
   - Business process goals
3. **Business process management concepts and fundamentals** (10%) $\Rightarrow$ Chapter 4:
   - Function-centric vs. process-centric organization
   - Characteristics of process management
   - Advancements in process management
   - Stakeholders' roles and responsibilities
   - Enabling tools of process management
4. **Business motivation modeling** (16%) $\Rightarrow$ Chapter 5:
   Business Modeling Fundamentals and Elements of the *Business Motivation Model* (BMM):
   - Vision, goals, objectives
   - Means and ends
   - Mission, strategies, tactics
   - Aspects of business modeling
5. **Business process modeling concepts** (24%) $\Rightarrow$ Chapter 6:
   This section is based on *Business Process Model and Notation 2.0* (BPMN 2.0):
   - BPMN basics
   - Definition of all diagram elements of BPMN (descriptive and analytical)

- Activities
- Grouping diagram elements

6. **Business process modeling skills** (16%) ⇒ Chapter 6:
   This section is also based on BPMN. Instead of basic concepts, it examines the ability to understand these concepts. Most questions in this section ask something about a brief scenario presented, either as a BPMN diagram, or in a few sentences. The focus is on all BPMN elements at the descriptive and analytical level.

7. **Process quality, governance, and metrics frameworks** (15%) ⇒ Chapter 7:
   This section examines the awareness of frameworks in the area of reference models, quality standards, metrics, and governance frameworks. Covered frameworks include:
   - *APQC Process Classification Framework* (PCF)
   - *Supply Chain Operation Reference Model* (SCOR)
   - *Value Chain Reference Model* (VRM)
   - *Business Process Maturity Model* (BPMM)
   - *Six Sigma*
   - *Balanced Scorecard*
   - *COBIT*
   - *Sarbanes-Oxley Act* (SOX)

A.1.1 **References**

There is no single book that covers all topic fields.[1] The references and the OMG specifications at http://www.omg.org/oceb-2/coveragemap-fund.htm are also part of the coverage map. They include concrete contents on the seven topic fields and are the source of the exam questions.

A.2 **SOLUTIONS**

See Tables A.1 to A.6.

Table A.1 Solutions Chapter 2: Basic Principles of Business Management

1	b	2	c
3	b	4	a
5	b	6	b
7	d	8	c
9	b		

---

[1]Except, of course, this preparatory book that you're holding in your hands right now.

Table A.2 Solutions Chapter 3: Business Processes

1	a	2	c
3	b	4	c
5	b	6	c
7	b	8	d

Table A.3 Solutions Chapter 4: Business Process Management

1	d	2	c
3	a	4	c
5	b	6	d

Table A.4 Solutions Chapter 5: Business Modeling

1	c	2	d
3	b	4	a
5	a	6	c
7	a	8	b
9	c	10	b
11	a		

Table A.5 Solutions Chapter 6: Modeling Business Processes Using BPMN

1	d	2	a
3	a	4	b
5	b	6	c
7	b	8	d
9	c	10	d
11	b	12	c

Table A.6 Solutions Chapter 7: Frameworks

1	c	2	a
3	c	4	b
5	a	6	b
7	c	8	d
9	c	10	c
11	b	12	d

Glossary

A

Abstract syntax The abstract syntax is a system of rules according to which permitted constructions are formed from the basic terminology of a language.

Activity An activity is a step in a ⇒ business process that has no further details.

Activity (BPMN) An activity describes a job within a ⇒ business process.

Activity type (BPMN) An activity type describes a special behavior of an ⇒ activity, and can be identified using a custom symbol. Predefined activity types are ⇒ loop task, ⇒ multiple instance, ⇒ *ad hoc* subprocess, ⇒ transaction, and ⇒ compensation.

***Ad hoc* subprocess (BPMN)** The *ad hoc* subprocess comprises ⇒ activities that are executed randomly—without a predefined sequence.

American Productivity and Quality Center *American Productivity and Quality Center* (APQC) is a nonprofit organization that offers assessments and best practices for business processes. APQC is the publisher of ⇒ *Process Classification Framework*.

Appraisal team (BPMM) The appraisal team determines the conformity of a ⇒ business process on the maturity level of the ⇒ BPMM.

APQC American Productivity and Quality Center

Artifact (BPMN) An artifact is a graphical element that contains additional process or element information, but doesn't influence the flow directly. Artifacts include ⇒ groups and ⇒ text annotations.

Assessment (BMM) The assessment assesses the neutral ⇒ influencers on goals and the ⇒ means used.

Association (BPMN) The association connects ⇒ artifacts with other model elements.

B

Balanced Scorecard The *Balanced Scorecard* (BSC) is a ⇒ management framework that compares key figures with the ⇒ vision and ⇒ strategies of an enterprise.

BAM Business Activity Monitoring

Best practice A best practice is the best approach to implement something based on experience.

Black Belt *Black Belt* is a role in a ⇒ Six Sigma project, and titles an experienced Six Sigma user who usually manages Six Sigma projects.

BMM Business Motivation Model

BPEL4WS Business Process Execution Language for Web Services

BPM Business Process Management

BPMI Business Process Management Initiative

BPMM Business Process Maturity Model

BPMN Business Process Model and Notation

BPR Business Process Reengineering

Break-even analysis The *break-even analysis* calculates the ⇒ break-even point.

Break-even point The break-even point describes the quantity of a product where the sales revenues cover the production costs (the intersection of the quantity-dependent cost line and the revenue line). If more products are sold, this results in profit. If less products are sold, this results in loss.

BSC Balanced Scorecard

Business Activity Monitoring *Business Activity Monitoring* (BAM) refers to the computer-aided collection, formatting, and presentation of business process data in real time.

Business administration *Business administration* entails the governing and organizing of business activities.

Business function The business function is a group of related tasks of an enterprise.

Business Motivation Model The *Business Motivation Model* (BMM) is a standard of ⇒ OMG and describes, on the one hand, the ⇒ desired results of an enterprise with a superior ⇒ vision and, on the other hand, the associated implementation strategies and tactics with their superior ⇒ missions.

Business policy The business policy is a set of ⇒ organizational policies. Synonym: Business policy.

Business process A business process is a business flow.

Business Process Analysis (BPA) The Business Process Analysis (BPA) detects implicit process knowledge and provides it.

Business Process Engine A *Business Process Engine* is an application for executing processes. Here, the engine executes a defined sequence of ⇒ activities.

Business Process Execution Language for Web Services A *Business Process Execution Language for Web Services* (BPEL4WS) is an XML-based language for describing ⇒ business processes, whose individual ⇒ activities are implemented by web services.

Business Process Management Abbreviation BPM

Business Process Management (BPM) Business process management comprises coordinated tasks to record, improve, and integrate processes of the organization. In this context, the organization is considered as a system of linked processes.

Business Process Management Initiative A *Business Process Management Initiative* (BPMI) is a non-profit organization founded in 2000 with the goal of developing standards in the business process area. In 2005, BPMI merged with ⇒ OMG.

Business Process Management Suite A *Business Process Management Suite* (BPMS) is a collection of IT applications for supporting ⇒ business process management.

Business Process Maturity Model The *Business Process Maturity Model* (BPMM) is a five-level ⇒ maturity model for ⇒ business processes of ⇒ OMG.

Business Process Model and Notation *Business Process Model and Notation* (BPMN) is a graphical modeling language of ⇒ OMG for describing ⇒ business processes.

Business Process Reengineering *Business Process Reengineering* (BPR) is a radical approach that propagates the new development of ⇒ business processes instead of their adaptation. It was presented by Michael Hammer and James Champy in the 1990s.

Business strategy The business strategy defines the direction into which an organization develops.

C

Capability Maturity Model *Capability Maturity Model* (CMM) is a ⇒ maturity model for software development processes.

Capability Maturity Model Integration Capability Maturity Model Integration (CMMI) replaced CMM in 2003 and addresses further disciplines, such as systems engineering, in addition to software development.

CMM Capability Maturity Model

CMMI Capability Maturity Model Integration

COBIT Control Objectives for Information and related Technology

Collaboration business process The collaboration business process describes the orchestration of an interaction, that is an exchange, like in public business processes, and additionally describes the detailed process steps, if required.

Collapsed subprocess (BPMN) The collapsed subprocess refers to a separate diagram that contains the detailed flow of the ⇒ subprocess.

Compensation (BPMN) Compensation is an explicit reverse action of ⇒ activities that were performed successfully.

Complex gateway (BPMN) In a complex gateway, the sequence flow runs along one or more borders, depending on the complex branch condition.

Concrete syntax The concrete syntax is the (textual or graphical) representation of an ⇒ abstract syntax. Synonym: notation.

Conditional sequence flow (BPMN) The conditional ⇒ sequence flow is a sequence flow that comes directly from an ⇒ activity and has a condition.

Connecting object (BPMN) The connecting object is either a ⇒ sequence flow, a ⇒ message flow, or an ⇒ association that connects ⇒ flow objects.

Control objective The control objectives are areas that must be considered in a process in order to achieve the process goal.

Control Objectives for Information and related Technology *Control Objectives for Information and related Technology* (COBIT) is a ⇒ governance framework of ⇒ ISACA that links enterprise-wide governance frameworks with IT.

Corporate governance Corporate governance is the set of all applicable rules, provisions, values, and principles for designing, governing, and monitoring the enterprise.

Corporate Social Responsibility *Corporate Social Responsibility* (CSR) entails the corporate responsibility toward society, which goes beyond the statutory requirements.

Critical path The critical path is the sequence of activities in a ⇒ network plan with the highest cumulated duration. If an activity in the critical path is delayed, the finish date of the network plan is delayed as well.

Critical Success Factor The *Critical Success Factor* (CSF) is a property that is necessary to achieve a specific goal.

CRM Customer Relationship Management

Crossover analysis The crossover analysis compares different scenarios with regard to ⇒ fixed costs and ⇒ variable costs.

CSF Critical Success Factor

CSR Corporate Social Responsibility

CTX CTX is a quality characteristic in ⇒ Six Sigma. CT stands for *critical to*, and the X is in the place of the characteristic.

Current assets The current assets are the assets that are available at short notice.

Current liability The current liabilities include all debts that must, or will be, cleared within 1 year.

Customer Relationship Management *Customer Relationship Management* (CRM) refers to the systematic design of customer relationship processes.

D

Data association A data association connects a ⇒ data object with a ⇒ flow object (⇒ activity, ⇒ gateway, or ⇒ event) or a ⇒ sequence flow.

Data object (BPMN) A data object is a business object that can be generated, required, changed, or destroyed by an ⇒ activity. Moreover, it can have a specific state.

Data Warehouse A *Data Warehouse* is a central, integrated data storage.

Data-based exclusive gateway (BPMN) The data-based ⇒ exclusive gateway decides, depending on the conditions in the ⇒ sequence flow, how the ⇒ token migrates.

Decision tree The decision tree is a hierarchical visualization of decision rules and paths.

Default sequence flow (BPMN) The default sequence flow receives the ⇒ token whenever no condition of the other outgoing ⇒ sequence flows is met.

Defects per Million Opportunities The quality methodology of ⇒ Six Sigma defines the quality measure, *Defects per Million Opportunities* (DPMO), which indicates the number of possible errors in one million opportunities.

Desired result (BMM) The desired result is a superordinate for ⇒ goals and ⇒ objectives.

E

EDM Enterprise Decision Management

End (BPMN) The end describes the ⇒ vision of the enterprise, and the goals and objectives derived thereof.

End event (BPMN) The end event ends the execution of the process and marks the process end.

Enterprise Decision Management *Enterprise Decision Management* (EDM) refers to the design of partly automated decision rules of an enterprise with reference to customer, employee, and supplier relationships.

Enterprise Resource Planning *Enterprise Resource Planning* (ERP) is the targeted deployment of enterprise resources for an optimal flow of ⇒ business processes.

Enterprise Service Bus *Enterprise Service Bus* (ESB) is an information technology for integrating a distributed application landscape into an enterprise.

EPC Event-Driven Process Chain

ERP Enterprise Resource Planning

ESB Enterprise Service Bus

Event (BPMN) An event is something that happens during a ⇒ business process and starts, ends, delays, or interrupts the flow.

Event-based exclusive gateway (BPMN) Depending on the incoming ⇒ event, the *event-based ⇒ exclusive gateway* decides which flow is continued.

Event-driven process chain The *Event-Driven Process Chain* (EPC) is a flowchart from the ARIS tool and methodology.

Exclusive gateway (BPMN) An *exclusive ⇒ gateway* restricts the ⇒ sequence flow in such a way that exactly one alternative is selected from a set of alternatives at runtime.

Expanded subprocess (BPMN) The inside of the expanded subprocess includes the detailed flow of the ⇒ subprocess.

F

Fixed costs Fixed costs are costs that are constant within a specific period of time, and are independent of the production volume or quantity of sales.

Flow object (BPMN) The flow object is an ⇒ event, ⇒ activity, or ⇒ gateway.

Framework The framework is a conceptual structure that supports the solution of complex problems.

G

Gateway (BPMN) The gateway controls how the ⇒ sequence flow spreads and merges within a process.

Goal The goal elaborates the ⇒ vision of an organization, that is, it describes the long-term goal that must be achieved in order to enhance the vision.

Governance framework The governance framework specifies how processes can be governed.

GRC Governance, Risk, and Compliance

Green Belt *Green Belt* is a leader in a ⇒ Six Sigma project.

Group (BPMN) The group combines multiple elements that logically belong together.

Guideline The guideline is a set of ⇒ principles.

H

Heat Map The heat map shows volatile data in a two-dimensional graphic, in which the values are displayed in different colors.

I

Inclusive gateway (BPMN) In an inclusive ⇒ gateway, the ⇒ sequence flow runs along one or more borders depending on the branch conditions.

Influencer (BMM) The influencer describes a condition that can result in changes to the ⇒ end, or ⇒ means of, an enterprise. An influencer can be internal (from within the enterprise) or external (from outside the enterprise boundaries).

Information Systems Audit and Control Association The *Information Systems Audit and Control Association* (ISACA) is an international, noncommercial organization that supports the examination, monitoring, and security of information systems.

Intermediate event (BPMN) The intermediate event occurs between the ⇒ start event and the ⇒ end event, and influences the flow.

ISACA Information Systems Audit and Control Association

ISO 9000 ISO 9000 standards specify a set of ⇒ guidelines for quality improvement.

IT Governance Institute The *IT Governance Institute* (ITGI) was founded by ⇒ ISACA in 1998 to advance the development of international standards for the administration and control of enterprise-internal information systems.

IT Infrastructure Library *IT Infrastructure Library* (ITIL) is a collection of ⇒ best practices for the implementation of an IT service management.

ITGI IT Governance Institute

ITIL IT Infrastructure Library

K

Key Performance Indicator The *Key Performance Indicator* (KPI) is a business ⇒ metric that measures the degree of fulfillment of a goal or a ⇒ CSF.

KPI Key Performance Indicator

L

Lane (BPMN) A lane structures the ⇒ activities within a ⇒ pool.

Loop task (BPMN) The loop task, or loop subprocess, describes executions that are repeated until the loop condition is met.

Lower Control Limit (LCL) (Six Sigma) The lower control limit defines the lower limit of a quality characteristic that differentiates between normal and abnormal deviation.

M

Management The term *management* describes the process of letting things happen by others.

Management framework The management framework specifies ⇒ best practices, ⇒ guidelines, and tools that support ⇒ the management in its management and monitoring tasks.

Manager The *manager* is a person who organizes, plans, supports, defines, and assesses the work of others.

Marketing *Marketing* is the market-oriented realization of enterprise goals, and the alignment of the entire enterprise in the market.

Master Black Belt *Master Black Belt* is an experienced ⇒ Six Sigma expert who works as a coach and trainer of the Six Sigma project.

Maturity model The maturity model is a model for assessing the quality of something.

MDA Model-Driven Architecture

Means (BMM) Means describe what the enterprise deploys to meet the enterprise object. This does not refer to employees or money, but to ⇒ missions, ⇒ strategies, and ⇒ tactics.

Message flow (BPMN) The message flow symbolizes the information that is exchanged between ⇒ participants.

Metric Metric refers to a measure system for the quantification of something.

Mission (BMM) The mission describes what an enterprise does to achieve a ⇒ vision.

Model-Driven Architecture (MDA) The model-driven architecture refers to a software development approach that separates the subject matter knowledge to be implemented from the necessary technology.

Multiple instance (BPMN) The multiple instance represents multiple parallel or sequential execution with different data.

N

Net income The net income is the remaining profit after tax and other charges.

Network plan The network plan is a graphical, network-like presentation of sequence-dependent and sequence-independent activities (including duration and the earliest and latest start and end date).

Notation Concrete syntax

O

Object Management Group *Object Management Group* (OMG) is a consortium of international enterprises that creates and publishes standards in the area of modeling and interoperability.

Objective The objective quantifies ⇒ goals. In other words, it makes them measurable.

OCEB2 OMG Certified Expert in Business Process Management 2

OMG Object Management Group

OMG Certified Expert in Business Process Management 2 *OMG Certified Expert in Business Process Management 2* (OCEB2) is a person who acquired a certification from the five-level OCEB certification program of ⇒ OMG.

Organizational control Organizational control is an activity which ensures that a directive, such as an ⇒ organizational policy or a ⇒ guideline, is adhered to.

Organizational policy The organizational policy is a formal document that describes the organization's attitude toward a specific aspect.

Organizational procedure An organizational procedure is a step-by-step instruction on how to implement a task.

Overhead costs Overhead costs are costs that can only be allocated indirectly to a cost unit (product, service).

Owner's equity The owner's equity is the part of the company assets that is left after the deduction of debt capital (noncurrent and ⇒ current liabilities).

P

Parallel gateway (BPMN) A parallel ⇒ gateway divides the ⇒ sequence flow into two or more parallel flows and then joins the parallel flows again. The synchronization waits until all incoming sequence flows have arrived. Only then is the flow continued.

Participant The participant is an enterprise, a customer, or a business partner, and is responsible for the execution of a process. In ⇒ BPMN, participants are mapped using ⇒ pools.

PCF Process Classification Framework

PEST analysis STEP analysis

Pool (BPMN) The pool represents a ⇒ participant, and serves as a container for the ⇒ sequence flow between ⇒ activities. Pools can contain ⇒ lanes.

Porter's Five Forces Porter's Five Forces support an enterprise in selecting a suitable strategy to gain a competitive advantage.

Principle A principle is a generally acknowledged rule.

Private business process The private business process contains only process steps that are executed within the organization.

Process Classification Framework *Process Classification Framework* (PCF) is a category model that categorizes a wide range of processes.

Process control plan (Six Sigma) The process control plan presents the process input parameters relevant for quality. See also ⇒ process management summary.

Process diagram The process diagram is a diagram type of ⇒ BPMN for representing ⇒ processes.

Process discovery The process discovery is a process for discovering implicit process knowledge.

Process Engine Business Process Engine

Process management summary Process management summary is a ⇒ Six Sigma tool of process monitoring that makes all critical process output parameters, which decide on the quality, visible and, therefore, manageable.

Process owner The process owner is responsible for the success of his process, and has appropriate rights and duties.

Process topology The process topology describes the structure of a process, that is the flow steps and their interrelations.

Production Rules Representation The *Production Rules Representation* (PRR) is a standard of ⇒ OMG for the manufacturer-independent presentation of production rules.

Program Manager (Six Sigma) The program manager is responsible for the introduction and implementation of ⇒ Six Sigma.

Project A project is an undertaking that is unique in its entirety, with limited timeframes and budget to deliver clearly defined results.

Project management Project management is the deployment of knowledge, skills, tools, and techniques in a project.

PRR Production Rules Representation

Public business process The public ⇒ business process describes the interaction between a ⇒ private business process and one or more other participants.

Q

Quality Quality means to meet the customer's requirements.

Quality control chart The quality control chart shows an individual-quality characteristic along a time-dependent course. It is a variant of the ⇒ run charts.

Quality framework The quality framework supports the improvement or management of a product or service's quality.

Quality management system The Quality Management System (QMS) specifies the structures, roles, resources, and processes that are necessary to implement an active ⇒ management of quality.

R

Regulation Regulation is a directive published by legislature, and compliance is mandatory. Punishments are possible if they are not complied with.

Return on Investment *Return on Investment* (ROI) is a financial key figure for assessing the profitability of an investment made. An investment is unprofitable if the net income made, divided by the used ⇒ owner's equity, is ≤1.0.

ROI Return on Investment

Role The role is the set of expectations toward a person.

Run chart The *run chart* is a two-dimensional graphic that illustrates the deviations of values from a specification along a time axis.

S

SaaS Software as a Service

Sarbanes-Oxley Act The Sarbanes-Oxley Act is a federal act that ensures the correctness and reliability of published financial data of enterprises whose stocks are on the US stock exchanges.

SBVR Semantics of Business Vocabulary and Rules

Semantics Semantics describes and explains the meaning of a term of a language.

Semantics Business Vocabulary and Rules *Semantics Business Vocabulary and Rules* (SBVR) are a standard of ⇒ OMG for describing business objects and business rules.

Sequence flow (BPMN) The sequence flow links the ⇒ flow objects, and, therefore, describes the flow sequence of ⇒ activities in the ⇒ process.

Service Level Agreement The *Service Level Agreement* (SLA) is a contract between a customer and a service provider, and defines the quality of interfaces.

Service-oriented architecture The Service-Oriented Architecture (SOA) is an approach for the implementation of ⇒ business processes in distributed systems, which is based on individual business functions.

Six Sigma Six Sigma is a methodology for improving processes in order to increase the quality of products and services.

Six Sigma Champion The Six Sigma Champion is a driver for the Six Sigma program. He or she establishes a new way of thinking and is responsible, for example, for assigning the Black Belt, Green Belt, and Yellow Belt roles.

SLA Service Level Agreement

SOA Service-Oriented Architecture

Software as a Service *Software as a Service* (SaaS) is a business model that provides software as a service.

Stakeholder The stakeholder is a person or institution that has an interest in a project and potentially contributes requirements.

Start event (BPMN) The start event triggers a ⇒ process and marks the beginning of the flow.

STEP analysis The STEP analysis provides references for considering the opportunities and threats of a market. Synonym: PEST analysis.

Strategy (BMM) The strategy channels efforts toward ⇒ goals.

Subject Matter Expert (SME) The subject matter expert is a person that has established professional expertise in a defined area.

Subprocess (BPMN) The subprocess is a combination of detailed ⇒ activities.

Swim lane (BPMN) A swim lane is a graphical container that separates a set of ⇒ activities from other activities. BPMN knows two types of swim lanes: ⇒ Pools and ⇒ Lanes.

SWOT analysis The SWOT analysis considers the internal strengths and weaknesses of an organization, and the external opportunities and risks in the market.

T

Tactic (BMM) The tactic implements ⇒ strategies.

Task (BPMN) The task is an atomic ⇒ activity within a ⇒ process, that is, the task is not detailed as a graphic in the model.

Terminate (BPMN) Terminate is the ⇒ trigger of an ⇒ end event that destroys all active ⇒ tokens and, therefore, ends the entire ⇒ process.

Text annotation (BPMN) The text annotation is a textual description that can be connected with every diagram element via an ⇒ association.

Token (BPMN) A token is some sort of virtual marble, which is generated when a process is called, and stands for, a concrete flow along ⇒ events, ⇒ activities, ⇒ gateways, and ⇒ sequence flows.

Total Quality Management *Total Quality Management* (TQM) is a methodology to improve the quality through active management of processes.

Toyota Production System The *Toyota Production System* (TPS) is a procedure for a series production developed by Toyota. The goal of TPS is the productivity of mass production in combination with the quality of shop production.

TPS Toyota Production System

TQM Total Quality Management

Transaction (BPMN) The transaction comprises multiple-work steps that collectively form an indivisible whole.

Trigger (BPMN) The trigger describes the cause as to why an ⇒ event occurs, and can be identified using custom symbols. Examples are message, timer, and ⇒ terminate.

U

Upper Control Limit (UCL) (Six Sigma) The upper control limit defines the upper limit of a quality characteristic that differentiates between normal and abnormal deviation.

V

Value chain The value chain represents the activities of an enterprise that are performed to design, produce, market, deliver, and support its product.

Value Chain Group Value Chain Group (VCG) is a nonprofit organization that develops and publishes the ⇒ *Value Reference Model*.

Value Reference Model The *Value Reference Model* (VRM) addresses the planning, management, and execution of ⇒ value chains in order to promote the effectiveness and optimization of processes.

Variable costs Variable costs are costs that vary if the production volume, or quantity of sales, changes.

VCG Value Chain Group

Vision (BMM) The vision is a meaningful, pictorial perception of the future of an enterprise that expresses an ultimate, rather unattainable, but desirable state.

VRM Value Reference Model

W

WfMC Workflow Management Coalition

Workflow Management Coalition *Workflow Management Coalition* (WfMC) is a coalition of manufacturers that develop and publish the workflow reference model, and other related standards.

Workflow pattern The workflow pattern is a solution guideline for describing a defined workflow sequence.

Working capital The *working capital* is part of the ⇒ current assets that is available for investments (after deduction of all debts that must be paid within 1 year).

Y

Yellow Belt *Yellow Belt* is a role in a ⇒ Six Sigma project that supports the ⇒ Green Belts and ⇒ Black Belts, and can manage small Six Sigma projects.

List of Literature

[1] Benner MJ, Tushman ML. Exploitation, exploration, and process management: the productivity dilemma revisited. Acad Manage Rev 2003;28:238–56.

[2] Business Motivation Model (BMM) Version 1.1. http://www.omg.org/spec/BMM/1.1; 2007.

[3] Business Process Maturity Model (BPMM) Version 1.0. http://www.omg.org/cgi-bin/doc?formal/08-06-01.pdf; 2008.

[4] Business Process Model and Notation (BPMN). http://www.omg.org/spec/BPMN/2.0/; 2011.

[5] American Productivity & Quality Center. APQC process classification framework, Version 6.0.0, http://www.apqc.org.

[6] Chang JF. Business process management systems. Boca Raton, FL: Auerbach Publications; 2006.

[7] Capability Maturity Model Integration (CMMI). http://www.sei.cmu.edu/cmmi/index.cfm.

[8] Workflow Management Coalition. Terminology & glossary. WFMC-TC-1011, 1999.

[9] Cougias DJ, et al. Say what you do: building a framework of IT controls, policies, standards, and procedures. Silicon Valley, CA: Shaser-Vartan; 2007.

[10] Supply-Chain Council. Supply Chain Council's supply-chain operations reference model (SCOR), Version 10.0, http://www.supply-chain.org.

[11] Davenport TH, Short JE. The new industrial engineering: information technology and business process redesign. Sloan Manage Review 1990;31:11–27.

[12] Deming WE. Report card on TQM. Manage Review January 1994;22–25.

[13] Gygi C, et al. Six sigma for dummies. 2nd ed. Hoboken, NJ: John Wiley & Sons; 2012.

[14] Dumas M, et al. Fundamental of business process management. Berlin, Heidelberg: Springer-Verlag; 2003.

[15] Fingar P. Systems thinking: the »core« core competency for BPM, BP Trends; September, 2005. http://www.bptrends.com/publicationfiles/09-05%20ART%20Systems%20Thinking%20-%20Fingar.pdf.

[16] Organisation for Economic Co-operation and Development. Guidelines for the security of information systems and networks; 2002, http://www.oecd.org/dataoecd/16/22/15582260.pdf.

[17] Gorman T. The complete idiot's guide to MBA basics. 2nd ed. Indianapolis, IN: Alpha Books; 2003.

[18] Object Management Group. Press release on the start of the OCEB certification program; 2008, http://www.omg.org/news/releases/pr2008/03-27-07.htm.

[19] Object Management Group, OMG Certified Expert in BPM. http://www.omg.org/oceb; 2009.

[20] Value Chain Group. Introduction to the value reference model (VRM); 2009, http://www.value-chain.org/en/cms/?1960.

[21] Hackmann JR, Wageman R. Total quality management: empirical, conceptual, and practical issues. Admin Sci Q 1995;40:309–42.

[22] Hall J. Overview of OMG business motivation model: core concepts; 2008, http://www.omg.org/oceb/BMM_Overview-Core_Concepts_[081208].pdf.

[23] Hammer M. Reengineering work: don't automate, obliterate. Harv Bus Rev 1990;68:104–12.

[24] Hammer M, Champy J. Business reengineering. A manifestation for business revolution. 7th ed. Frankfurt: Campus Fachbuch; 1996.

[25] Kaplan RS, Norton DP. The balanced scorecard: translating strategy into action. Boston, MA: Harvard Business School Press; 1996.

[26] Madison DJ. Becoming a process-focused organization, Westborough, MA: BPM Institute; 2007, http://www.bpminstitute.org/articles/article/article/becoming-a-process-focused-organization.html.

[27] Ould MA. Business process management: a rigorous approach. Tampa, FL: Meghan-Kiffer Press; 2005.

[28] Porter ME. Competitive advantage: creating and sustaining superior performance. New York, NY: Free Press; 2004.

[29] Rummler GA, Brache AP. Improving performance: how to manage the white space in the organization chart. 2nd ed. San Francisco, CA: Jossey-Bass; 1995.

[30] Siegel J. In OMG's OCEB certification program, what is the definition of business process; 2008, http://www.omg.org/oceb/defbusinessprocess.htm.

[31] Silver B. BPMN method and style. Aptos, CA: Cody-Cassidy Press; 2011.

[32] Silver B. Three levels of process modeling with BPMN. BPMS watch, 2008. April, http://www.brsilver.com/wordpress/subscribers-only-2/three-levels-of-process-modeling-with-bpmn.

[33] Smith A. The wealth of nations. Köln: Anaconda Verlag; 2009.

[34] Smith H, Fingar P. Business process management: the third wave. 4th ed. Tampa, FL: Meghan Kiffer Press; 2007.

[35] Stralser S. MBA in a day. Hoboken, NJ: John Wiley & Sons; 2004.

[36] A UML profile for MARTE. http://www.omg.org/cgi-bin/doc?realtime/07-03-03; 2007.

[37] Verner L. The challenge of process discovery, BPTrends, 2004. May, http://www.businessprocesstrends.com/deliver_file.cfm?fileType=publication&fileName=05-04_WP_Process_Discovery-Verner1.pdf.

[38] E. Walters. What are CSFs and KPIs? http://www.12manage.com/methods_rockart_csfs_kpis.html.

[39] Weilkiens T. Systems with SysML/UML. Morgan Kaufmann; 2008.

Index

Note: Page numbers followed by *f* indicate figures, and *ge* indicate glossary terms.